PLAN AND BUILD MORE STORAGE SPACE

PLAN AND BUILD MORE STORAGE SPACE

PETER JONES

Butterick Publishing

Book Design by Bobye List
Illustrations by Gary Tong

Library of Congress Cataloging in Publication Data
Jones, Peter, 1934–
    Plan and build more storage space.
    Includes index.
    1. Cabinet-work. 2. Clothes closets. 3. Shelving (Furniture)
    4. Storage in the home. I. Title.
TT197.J655   684.1'6   79-10386
ISBN 0-88421-036-7

Copyright © 1979 by
Butterick Publishing
708 Third Avenue
New York, New York 10017
A Division of American Can Company

Manufactured and printed in the United States of America.
Published simultaneously in the USA and Canada.

Table of Contents

ONE

Storage and the Space It Uses

THE IDEAL STORAGE IS A PLACE TO KEEP OUR POSSESsions out of the way when we don't need them, but readily accessible when we want to use them. That seems simple enough except that most people usually wind up just getting their possessions out of the way. Closets become stuffed with clothing, linen and all manner of other objects that are buried under and behind each other for so long their owners forget they even possess them. Shelves become receptacles for everything and anything that will fit on them and eventually become so cluttered that nobody dares to look on them for anything. Bookcases groan under tons of printed paper, with books jammed behind and on top of each other until they are impossible to locate when they are needed. Cabinets are blessed with doors that can mercifully be closed over the debris that is crammed behind them. But it is that door, which presents a neat, orderly face to the world, that makes most cabinets useless as far as retrieval of their contents is concerned. Indeed, cabinets can become so overloaded that it is positively dangerous for anyone to open them.

The problem with most storage space is primarily a human condition: out of sight, out of mind. When the season is over, toss the ski equipment someplace where it will not be in the way for six months and it does not really matter where you put it. That applies to many of our possessions, particularly the ones that we need only part of the time. Don't feel guilty. Everybody tends to store things the same way, inconvenient as that is for our day-to-day living.

The way around all this is to construct storage space so that it cannot be misused. Thus, if a cabinet is intended to hold dry goods or cans, make the shelves just large enough to hold all of your dry goods and cans, and nothing more. Actually, you will quickly discover that if you design a storage area to hold particular objects, you will need less storage space than you originally imagined. It is perhaps helpful, when considering your storage needs, to ask yourself two basic questions:

1. *How often do you need a particular object?* Your toaster or coffeepot is used every morning. Christmas tree ornaments are taken out of their boxes once a year. Sports equipment is used for perhaps six months and then put away for the other half of the year.

There are three kinds of storage space: live, dead and occasional; and which articles are placed in which space depends on how often you use them. *Live* storage is for anything you use practically every day. Consequently, it is usually located in the primary living areas of your home, such as the kitchen, bedrooms or bathroom. The kind of things you might place in live storage are books, records, tools, cosmetics, food and cooking implements.

Dead storage is, logically enough, the opposite of live storage, and is relegated to out-of-the-way parts of the house, such as the attic, garage or basement. The possessions that you put in dead storage are things you use once a decade, or at best once a year, so they do not have to be very accessible. Your Christmas tree stand, fur coat, old army boots and inherited quasi-antiques usually wind up in dead storage.

Occasional storage is space designed to hold seasonal objects. The major problem with occasional storage is the diversity of what it must hold—articles as oddly shaped as a punch bowl, skis, leaf rakes, insect repellent and lawn mowers.

The storage that you build divides into two specific types: open and closed. *Open* storage is comprised of shelves or any level platform that permits you to display your most prized possessions—books, plates, objets d'art. If they are not particularly prized, they are probably needed on a daily basis; the appliances that stand on that shelf you refer to as your kitchen counter are always readily accessible.

Closed storage is anything with a door on it—cabinets or their larger versions, closets. One advantage of closed storage is that by closing the door you can immediately forget all that clutter inside.

2. *Should the objects be stored permanently or temporarily?* If you are someone who packs up and moves every two or three years to a new apartment or house, you need to have storage units that can be assembled and disassembled with relative ease. The units can be made of almost any material, including cardboard, but typically they should be either freestanding or easily hung—and removed—from almost any wall.

Permanent storage may look like temporary storage but is to remain installed forever in the place it resides. Permanent storage includes most built-ins and as such is designed to take away a minimum amount of living space. It can, in fact, be constructed so that it is completely hidden from view or at least looks as if it were an integral part of its surroundings. The great advantage to permanent storage units is that they can be constructed in or around, or utilizing, existing walls, corners or other space.

PLANNING STORAGE

Nobody ever has enough storage space, even if it is totally organized and maintained. So from time to time everybody has to hunt around for some new, unobtrusive area that can be utilized for storing something. When you are planning storage space you have four basic objectives:

1. To create the most storage using the least possible space.
2. To allow articles to be easily put away and be just as easily accessible.
3. To protect the goods you store from breakage, dampness, heat, cold and rodents.
4. To create the storage area so that it does not take away from the attractiveness of its surroundings.

It helps considerably if you view every corner, every wall, the floors and even your ceilings not as so many flat surfaces, but as cubic spaces. A cabinet or shelf can be hung from a wall or the ceiling, and suddenly that flat surface becomes the back or top of a useful storage area. Look up at the ceiling of a closet and consider how much wasted, or at least unused, storage space is above your head—space that could hold a second clothing rod, for example, if you merely lowered the existing rod about 2'. Consider a "dead" corner between two doorways. It could contain shelves. It could also contain a standing cabinet with shelves against the walls as well as in the door, so that instead of nine deep storage platforms you have 18 narrower and probably more easily organized shelves that can all be closed from view.

You can completely enclose a doorway with bookshelves; the wall above and below a window can be used to support shelves or a cabinet. An alcove or any irregularity in a wall can be filled with shelves and sometimes given a door to create a closet. Even the triangular area under a stairway offers half a dozen opportunities for creating entirely usable storage space.

The remaining pages of this book contain a myriad of storage ideas. You may look at the drawings and discard them as unworkable for the space you have. Look again. Most likely if you change a shelf here, reverse the hinges on a cabinet there, reorganize the basic shape of a box somewhere else, you can find a way of fulfilling your storage needs. It becomes a kind of game you play with your possessions to see how many of them you can store in the smallest possible space and still not have any clutter, while maintaining accessibility to everything you own.

TWO

Designing Your Storage

SHELVES AND CABINETS

All storage is some form of shelf or cabinet. Shelves appear at first glance to be rather uncomplicated horizontal surfaces. But shelves occur in a dazzling array of variations. They can hang, slide, pop up, tilt or drop down; they can be recessed, cantilevered, revolving or designed in any number of other surprising forms; and you can make them out of practically any material, from concrete or metal to wood or plastic. But every shelf must have some form of stable vertical support; it must be securely attached to its verticals, and it must be strong enough to hold whatever weight it is expected to hold. It is fortunate if the shelf is also absolutely level, but that is not a prerequisite for its functioning successfully.

A cabinet is defined as an enclosed structure that is accessible through one of its sides. The open side may have a door that slides or is hinged, and the entire structure can be constructed from the same materials used to make shelves. You can hang a cabinet or let it be freestanding; it can be large or small, ornate or plain, movable or built-in. If it becomes so large you can stand in it, it is likely to be called a closet.

Hooks, Pegs and Hangers

Hooks, pegs and hangers could be classified as shelves, and they certainly present countless storage opportunities. They can be de-

11.

Shelves can slide on tracks (A), rotate on axles (B), form a separate insert in cabinets (C), hang from a wall (D), or be supported by brackets attached to the back of vertical 2×4s fixed between floor and ceiling (E).

Cabinets can take any shape and may incorporate any of the basic storage elements.

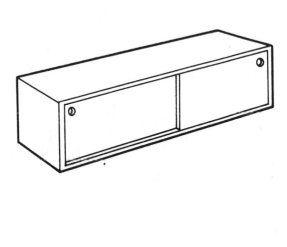

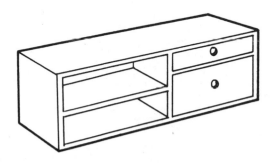

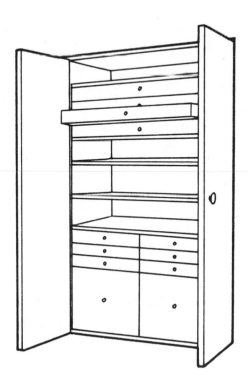

Aside from the basic wooden or metal dowel, hooks and hangers assume an astounding number of shapes.

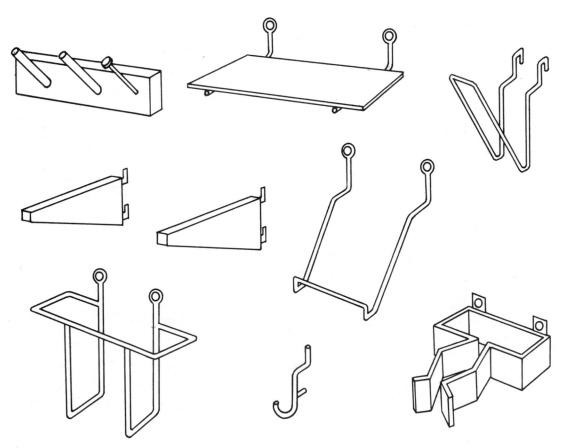

signed to hang bicycles, clothing, shelves, tools—practically any-thing—so they are always a worthwhile consideration when you have an object or group of objects that are hard to store in any other way, or if space is limited.

Boxes and Bins

Boxes are old standbys and are really just containers that must be reached into. They include baskets, hampers, tubs and chests, all of which may or may not have a lid. They are ideal for storing large quantities of things, but because they are often reluctant to make their contents accessible, they are more useful for occasional or dead storage than for live storage. You can do some marvelous tricks with boxes and bins, however. The rectangular plastic kind, for example, has a lipped rim that allows it to be hung between two pieces of wood so you can pull it out of a cabinet as you would a drawer. If you use the transparent plastic type you can hold it up over your head and see all the goodies you have carefully buried in the bottom of it. The colored plastic bins make good storage drawers for vegetables or fruit and can be hung inside an under-the-counter cabinet. You can also stack boxes with their open sides facing you, creating a whole wall of cubicles that will store all manner of possessions.

Boxes can be arranged in all sorts of decorative and utilitarian ways.

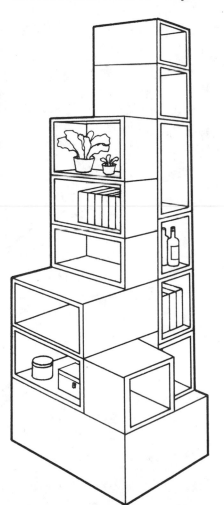

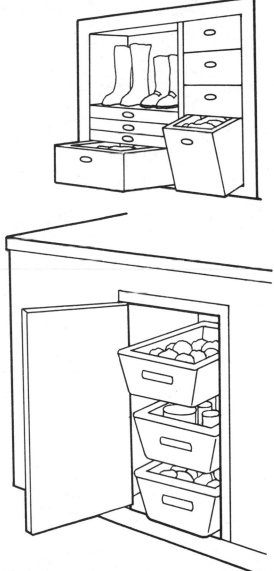

Drawers

As a form of box or bin, drawers offer the specific advantage of bringing their contents out of whatever space they reside in, and conveniently presenting them to the user. Essentially, a drawer is simply a box, even though it may have a decorative front and a mechanism that allows it to be pulled out of its space, which can be metal tracks or merely two pieces of smooth wood. Not only can you make

Drawers do not have to take their traditional form; they can be extremely shallow or they can be vertical. They can slide on wooden runners, metal tracks or even casters.

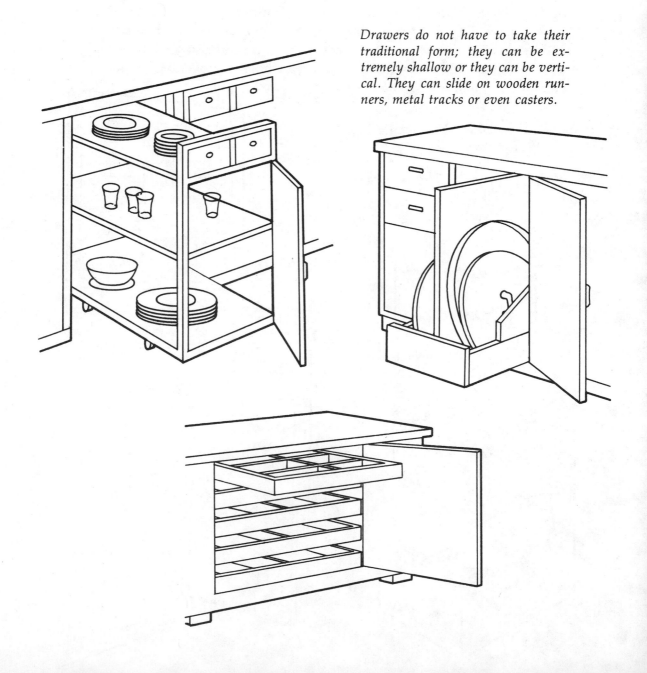

drawers of any size and material you wish, but you can also buy them in any number of stock sizes with or without something that is known as a drawer chest. A drawer chest is a frame that drawers fit into but that often comes without a back, sides or top. A ready-made chest can be inserted into whatever built-in arrangement you are constructing and, although it is more expensive than building the drawers and frame yourself, it can save you considerable time and frustration. Among cabinetmakers, drawer-making is considered about the testiest of all construction jobs, primarily because a really time-worthy drawer should be assembled with dadoes (grooves) or dovetail joints and be absolutely square in all directions.

There are some common-sense rules that should be observed with drawers. A drawer should be placed so that it can be pulled as far out as it will go without falling to the floor. It should have enough space in front of it so that the user can stand squarely before it. Drawers are normally about 12" deep, and while they can be as wide as you wish, the handles should be no more than 36" apart, which is a comfortable reach for most people. Few drawers are more than 30" deep, which is the reach of a long arm.

Closets

Technically, a closet is a small room or at least a recess in a wall, usually closed off with a curtain or some form of door that may slide, roll, fold or be hung. Ideal clothes closet depths are between 21" and 30"; you must have a minimum depth of 22" if you intend to hang clothes from a hanger in the closet. If the closet is intended for linens or cleaning equipment, between 12" and 16" should be enough; a closet 24" deep is adequate for holding sporting equipment, most luggage, bedding, card tables, folding chairs and other bulky items.

The trick to getting the most storage out of your closets is to view them as big boxes and remember that the space near their ceilings, which may be somewhat inaccessible, is a good place for a considerable amount of dead storage.

Closets can be carved out of any existing space, and their interiors organized for storing practically anything.

THE PLANNING PROCESS

Shelves, cabinets, hooks, hangers, pegs, boxes, bins, drawers and closets are the storage elements you have to work with when you begin to create more storage space in your home. No matter what you design or how you arrange your storage, you will always fill the space with some form of these nine elements. But which of them you use and how you arrange them are dictated by what you need to store and how accessible you want it to be.

Storage is most efficient when it is designed to hold specific objects—but don't go overboard with that idea. Don't make a compartment for every single item you own. In the first place, that will take tremendous amounts of time and money. Secondly, if you build an area for some object and then discard the item, what keeps the compartment from becoming wasted space? So flexibility is important in your thinking and designing of storage.

A built-in cabinet or storage area can be glorious. It can be designed to take up otherwise useless space and practically disappear into its surroundings, and still be eminently suitable for holding whatever it is designed to hold. But you can also overdo the notion of built-ins. An attractive freestanding cabinet can be moved around whenever you want to change the complexion of the room you put it in.

Measuring: The First Step

Even if you intend to go out and buy a storage unit, your first step is to measure the space you have available for storing things. Measure the width, depth and height of the walls that will surround the storage and also any protrusions (such as pipes or, most certainly, the wall baseboard) in the area. What you now have are the *outside* dimensions of the storage unit. If you are going to buy the unit, take all those protrusions well into account. If some vertical pipes extend 3" away from the back wall and the side walls are 24" deep, the back of your unit must either be notched out to allow for the pipes, or be no more than 21" deep.

If you are doing your own construction work and have the outside dimensions in hand, you can now subtract the thickness of the material you plan to use for the sides, back and front, top and bottom. If you are using wood, subtract between ½" and ¾" from each dimension, so that if your space is 18" wide and you are assembling a bookcase with ¾"-thick sides, the real length of the shelves will be:

18" minus ¾" minus ¾" (or 18" minus 1½") equals 16½".

When you have subtracted all of the wall thicknesses from your outside dimensions, you have arrived at the real dimensions of your storage space. Now the fun begins.

More Questions of Design

What exactly will be stored in this space? If the answer is several different kinds of things, measure the largest and the smallest objects. Somewhere in the storage unit you will have to make room for both, and exactly where you place them depends on where they will waste the minimum amount of space.

But there are other questions to consider: Can you have more shelves? Would a drawer or hangers be more efficient? Must all the shelves be the same width? Could they be shallower, with a door that has its own set of shelving for smaller objects? Should the storage be open or closed? If it is closed, how much storage area will you lose by the thickness of the door? Can the ceiling of the room be used in some manner? Keep asking yourself questions and answering them. Never stop asking, never quit trying to rearrange things in your mind; it is intriguing how often you will think you have arrived at the optimum only to discover that there is yet a better way of making the storage more versatile, more convenient or more useful.

At some point you can put your ruminations aside long enough to consider the construction itself. Start with more questions: What materials do you need? How will the pieces be assembled? Do you have the proper tools and materials to complete the project? If not, where can you beg, borrow or buy them? Do you have enough time to complete the project? With almost any project involving wood, take your estimated working time and double or triple it. You may surprise yourself and need less time, but more often some unexpected complication will arise during the construction that slows you down.

Drawing Plans

You do not have to be a mechanical engineer to sketch a plan of what you intend to build. The lines don't even need to be straight. The reason for doing any drawing at all is so that you will not forget the dimensions and positioning of pieces that you thus far have kept only in your head. Every line in your drawing should have its dimensions marked for your reference.

One very helpful tool to use for sketching projects is graph paper, which you can purchase at any stationery store. The paper is divided into ¼″ squares, so four of them equal an inch. The squares can be used as an automatic scale (say, one square equals 1′), saving you a lot of time counting half inches. Finally, they just plain make it easier to sketch any project in proportion.

Your drawing will be useful first when you begin to estimate your material needs and their cost, and second when you begin construction. You may also find that once you have drawn the project, your original ideas about shelf or drawer, hook or cabinet placement can be improved upon. Don't hesitate to redo your design. Also, do more than one view of it. A front view is mandatory. A side view is extremely useful, and sometimes a top or bottom view will help as well. Include all dimensions in each view.

The most important element to include when sketching a project is its dimensions. However, making sketches is considerably easier if you do them on graph paper, which provides squares that can be used to establish a scale.

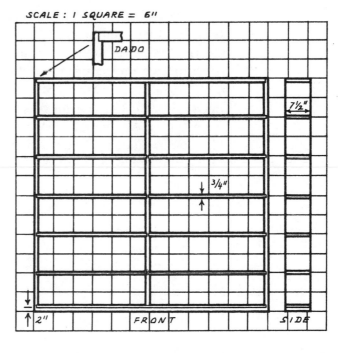

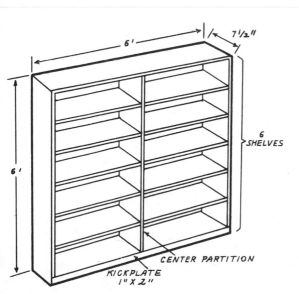

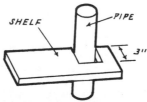

B.O.M.

Having developed your idea of a storage area, planned it on paper and given it both form and dimension, you can now work out a Bill of Materials. The B.O.M. must include the name of each part, the finished sizes of each part (thickness, width and length), the number of pieces and all the other materials such as hardware, paint, sandpaper, glue, etc., that you will need.

When you have detailed all of the pieces and their dimensions, divide them according to their thicknesses and widths, and add up their lengths. Suppose for a shelf case you need two side supports that are ¾" thick × 9½" wide × 96" long. Added together you will need a 16' length of wood that is ¾" thick and 9½" wide. When you have assembled all of the pieces on paper so that you know how many feet of each width and thickness you need, call your local lumberyard and ask for current prices. The price of wood is outrageous these days. It changes so fast (always going up, of course) that last week's lumber bill has no bearing on what you will pay today. The prices will be given to you as so much per foot or so much per board foot, or, in the case of plywood, so much per panel. Take those numbers and multiply them by the overall number of feet that you intend to purchase. Then add up all the numbers and that will give you your lumber cost. When building wooden storage units, you should also figure on buying about 15% more lumber than planned because of waste, spoilage and pieces that for one reason or another must be recut or replaced. Your projected costs should also include a complete listing of any hardware—knobs, hinges, catches, etc.—and their prices, together with what you expect to spend for nails, glue, screws and sandpaper.

The format for a Bill of Materials.

NO. OF PIECES	DIMENSIONS			KIND OF MATERIAL	NUMBER OF: BD. FT. SQ. FT. OR LIN. FT.	COST PER: BD. FT. SQ. FT. OR LIN. FT.	TOTAL COST
	T	W	L				

THREE

Wood–the Major Storage Material

THE PRIMARY MATERIALS YOU WILL NEED TO BUILD storage space in your home are wood, sandpaper, nails and adhesive. Sometimes screws, perhaps plastic laminate (Formica covering), bolts and, occasionally, various wall hangers are needed. In most instances, the major portion of your storage project does not need to look magnificent as long as it is strong and stable.

SOLID WOODS

You can buy lumber only in standard sizes, and with the cost of wood running on a par with sirloin steak, you don't want to buy any more of it than you absolutely need. So try to buy sizes that you can divide into the lengths you need with a minimum of waste. With some judicious measuring, you may even be able to get by with less than your 15% waste allowance. Most of the lumber you will use for your shelves or cabinets doesn't have to be top-grade, kiln-dried boards without knots. You're in luck if the wood doesn't happen to be warped or twisted, but these days even high-priced stock is, by the standards of 10 years ago, inferior. In any case, go the cheaper route with anything that is to become a shelf. You want the wood to be planed smooth on at least one side, but you can live with knots and even some minor splits.

Lumber Sizes

When you order shelving you are dealing with pine or fir boards which are designated as 1″ by a width of 2″, 3″, 4″, 6″, 8″, 10″, 12″, 14″, 16″ or 18″. Standard boards are sold in 8′ to 20′ lengths at 2′ intervals. But the wood you cart home from your local lumberyard is never 1″×6″, 1″×10″ or any other even number. Those are the *nominal* lumber sizes and all they tell you is how big the board was when it was rough-sawed at the lumber mill. It was then planed (surfaced) on both sides and both edges. Planing reduces the board thickness from 1″ to ¾″ and the width to ½″ less than the nominal width. Thus, if you order a 1″×8″ board you will receive one that is actually ¾″×7½″. It is important to remember the *real* dimensions of wood when you are computing the amount of space you intend to fill.

Most boards are priced by the linear foot, but occasionally you will run into the term "board foot," which is another way of computing the cost of wood. A board foot is 144 cubic inches. A piece of wood 12″ square by 1″ thick equals 1 board foot. It could also be 2″ thick by 6″ wide by 12″ long, or any other combination that adds up to 144 cubic inches. Once again, when wood is sold by the board foot it is computed according to the nominal, not the real, dimensions.

Working with Solid Woods

Wood is a marvelous material with tremendous advantages as far as workability is concerned. You can saw it, nail it, glue it, carve it, shape it in a hundred ways.

There are some fundamental facts about wood to bear in mind. All wood has a grain which is identified by a series of irregular, darker lines in its surface. The lines pretty much parallel each other although they form an irregular pattern that progresses, as a rule, along the length of a given board. If you are cutting or sanding the wood in the direction of the pattern, you are working *with* the grain. If you are working with the wood at right angles to the pattern, you are working *across* or *against* the grain.

You will discover that doing any work with the grain is considerably easier than going across it. You can, in fact, split a board along its grain much more easily than you can break it across the grain. The darker lines in the grain tell you in which direction the fibers of the wood are running. If you insert a saw blade between those fibers it becomes relatively easy to separate them and push your way along the length of the board. However, a nail can divide the wood fibers every bit as easily as a saw blade; consequently, nails will not stay in the ends of a board very well. Wood simply has no holding power if a nail is driven between the fibers of its grain, and if the nail is large enough, the wood will split. Unfortunately, you are most likely to drive a nail into the end of the grain if you are putting up shelves, so you must resort to a number of subterfuges to keep the horizontal members of a storage project in place between their vertical supports (see page 103).

Wood itself is light, flexible and strong. It can support surprising amounts of weight without breaking—it will bend a lot instead. As a cardinal rule, never allow a shelf made of softwood to span more than 36" without some sort of center support.

CUTTING   You can hand-saw across a pine or fir board without any great difficulty because it is usually only a few inches wide. But cutting a board lengthwise can be tedious and not terribly accurate. You have a better chance of conserving your energy and making cleaner, more accurate cuts if you use a power saw, either hand-held or stationary.

DRILLING   Drilling into softwood is never hazardous or difficult, particularly if you use an electric drill. Even with hand drills there is no great problem, since the wood is basically a soft material. Softwoods will not often splinter or chip, and even a dull bit can easily make its way between the fibers.

JOINING   Making a joint with softwood is easy to accomplish, but most often you are dealing with at least one end grain that will not accept nails very well. Joints should always be made using glue as well as either nails or screws. Screws are a more reliable fastener if you have to drive into the ends of a board.

PLYWOOD

Not so long ago, plywood was cheaper than pine or fir boards, and if you owned a table saw and could rip a plywood board in your home workshop, it was often cheaper to buy plywood panels and cut them up into whatever widths you needed. Today plywood is more expensive than pine or fir, although sometimes you can use a ½"-thick piece of plywood in place of ¾" shelving boards and keep your costs down somewhat. If you use ½" plywood it must be thoroughly braced, not because it is weaker than solid wood, but because it bends more. Half-inch-thick plywood can, in fact, hold as much weight as ¾"-thick pine or fir; if you support a ½" plywood shelf at its ends and along its back or front, it will hold an equal weight without bending.

Plywood has been an increasingly popular building material for well over 30 years. Although it dates back to the turn of the century, it did not come into its own until after World War II, when builders discovered that a plywood panel offers tremendous advantages.

Plywood is, for example, equally strong in all directions, while solid wood is considerably weaker along its grain. If it is manufactured properly, plywood will not crack or split and should not warp. Recently, manufacturing processes have begun to slip and it is not unusual to discover that all of the expensive panels you have just purchased are warped. However, by the time you get a standard 4'×8' plywood panel cut into pieces and the pieces are nailed or screwed into place the warp will hardly be noticeable. Plywood will not shrink or swell very much when the weather changes, either, and it is easily worked and finished. In fact, panels are smoothed during manufacture to the point where they need little more than a light sanding before being finished.

Plywood is manufactured by first slicing logs into fitches (veneers). A fitch is made by rotating the log against sharp cutting knives which slice no more than a ⅛"-thick sheet of wood off the outer edge of the log. The log keeps rotating against the knives until it has been peeled like an onion. Then the fitches are trimmed to their largest possible size with a minimum of natural defects. Each fitch is subsequently sent through a long oven and heated to about 350°F to reduce the moisture content in the wood to less than 4% (all wood is dried before it is sold).

Plywood panels are made with either a solid core or by laying a number of fitches together to make a veneer core. The solid-core panels have a center made of kiln-dried lumber or particleboard with fitches glued to both sides of the core. Every fitch is placed with its grain running at right angles to the fitch above and below it. No matter whether the panel is solid core or veneer core, the fitches are glued on both sides and laid on top of each other until the desired panel thickness is attained. Then this wood sandwich is put in a hot press that exerts 200 or 300 pounds of pressure per square inch and cooks the wood to a temperature of 250°F. When it comes out of the hot press the fitches are permanently bonded together and the face veneers of the panel are then sanded. Because every fitch in a panel has its grain going at right angles to the fitches above and below it, the plywood is inherently strong and less susceptible to breakage or shrinking and swelling.

There are two drawbacks to plywood, both concerning its edges. Since a plywood panel is made up of three to nine pieces of wood, and because the two outside veneers are less than ⅛" thick, the edges of the wood are relatively fragile. It is very easy to chip them when they are being drilled, sawed, planed or even sanded. The other problem with plywood edges is decorative. By current standards of taste, the multiple layers are not attractive, so it is necessary to go to the extra labor of hiding the exposed edges.

How Plywood Is Sold

Plywood is sold in thicknesses of ⅛" to 1¼" with the most usual dimensions being ¼", ½", ⅝" and ¾". Panels are usually 48" wide, but you can find them in widths of 36" and 60" and in lengths of 5' to 12'; the most common panel size is 4'×8'.

You can also purchase plywood marked as either "exterior" or "interior" grade. The exterior version is made with a waterproof glue that is so weather resistant the panels can be used to make boats.

Interior-grade panels are assembled with a water-resistant glue that can withstand some dampness, but not much.

You will also discover a pair of letters stamped on each panel, which tell you how close to perfect the outsides of the panel are. The letter N indicates about as perfect a face veneer as you will ever run into. The veneer is smooth, has no defects and will accept any kind of finish. One step down from the exalted level of N is A, which is smooth but has small, neat surface repairs; it too will accept any finish. B is pretty smooth and has a few more repairs in its face veneer; it will also accept paint and varnish. C has some splits and knotholes. D has knotholes up to 2½″ in diameter, some splits and knots, and is rough. The panels are stamped A-D, B-C or whatever the two face veneers are judged to be, and are priced accordingly. If you are making shelves you could use a C-D panel if the shelves are not going to be seen by anybody; their strength is just as good as an A-A panel, which you might choose for a cabinet door. The sides of a cabinet could be A-B or even A-C, with the lesser of the two sides forming the interior of the unit. Once again, wood is expensive, so buy only what you need, and anytime you don't need beauty, buy a cheaper grade.

You have still another option when buying plywood. Some panels are made with hardwood face veneers. The hardwoods include oak, birch, maple and walnut, and they present some magnificent wood patterns that will accept a varnish or shellac finish. As far as storage making is concerned, use hardwood-veneered panels sparingly—perhaps for doors or cabinets. The price is getting so high that you may want to think twice about what and how much you buy. If you skip the hardwood, the panels you purchase will have either pine or fir face veneers, with the fir being a little less expensive since it is more reluctant to accept a finish.

Working with Plywood

Bearing in mind that, by itself, every plywood fitch is thin and therefore fragile, most of the rules to remember about working with plywood are aimed at preserving the face veneers and panel edges.

CUTTING   Whatever saw you use, make sure it is sharp. It should be noted immediately that a 4'×8' panel of ¾" plywood is an ungainly and heavy object. The first cut you make in it should be designed to get the panel down to a manageable size like 4'×4' or 2'×8'. Most lumberyards will make the first cut for you using professional machinery and proper work space. In fact, for a fee (anywhere from 10¢ to $1 a cut) the yard will saw a panel into any number of pieces you wish. The best reason for having the yard do your cutting is that if you do not have a power saw of any sort, hand-cutting plywood is long, mean work, particularly if you are going the full 8' length of the panel.

The face veneer can become chipped and gouged when you are sawing. So, depending on the type of saw you are using, place the good side of the panel—the side that will be seen—up or down to keep it away from the pull of the blades. Follow this guide:

Hand saw	Good side up
Radial arm saw	Good side up
Table saw	Good side up
Saber saw	Good side down
Hand power saw	Good side down

To minimize splintering, tack a thin strip of wood over the cutting line and saw through that as well as the panel.

DRILLING   Anytime you drill a hole in plywood it will splinter. The drill bit goes into the panel with no trouble, but when it breaks through the last, thin veneer it is bound to tear at the wood. There are two ways of avoiding splinters. You can drill halfway through one side of the panel, then turn the wood over and drill through the other side—this requires some careful measuring. The second way is to clamp a piece of wood against the back of the panel for support; you still may get some splintering, but it will be minimal.

PLANING AND SANDING   Most plywood face veneers do not require any vigorous sanding except along their cut edges. Whether

In many instances you can clamp pieces of scrap wood on both sides of your work before you plane it, to prevent the edges from splintering.

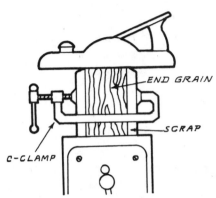
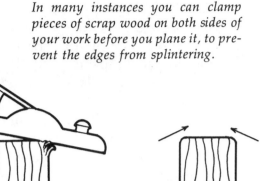
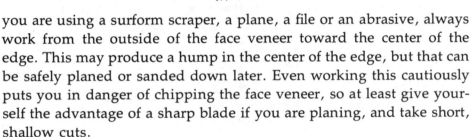

you are using a surform scraper, a plane, a file or an abrasive, always work from the outside of the face veneer toward the center of the edge. This may produce a hump in the center of the edge, but that can be safely planed or sanded down later. Even working this cautiously puts you in danger of chipping the face veneer, so at least give yourself the advantage of a sharp blade if you are planing, and take short, shallow cuts.

HIDING EDGES The faces of plywood rarely need any preparation for a finish besides the primer-sealer you use with any softwood. But plywood edges are literally sponges—they soak up any paint or varnish and look as if you had forgotten to cover them. So the edges must always be given special treatment. You can fill them with wood putty, plastic wood, spackle or wallboard compound. Or you can cover them with solid wood. You can tack a piece of molding or trim over them, or glue a strip of edging veneer to them. Edging veneer is sold in rolls at many larger hardware stores and is extremely thin ($1/42''$). You have to use contact cement or some other strong glue to hold it in place.

You can also rout out the center of the plywood edge or miter it, and insert a piece of wood in the groove or attach it to the mitered angle. These procedures require a tool like a table saw to cut the groove

The six ways of covering plywood edges. When nailing anything to an edge use long, thin finishing nails which are countersunk so that their heads can be covered with wood filler.

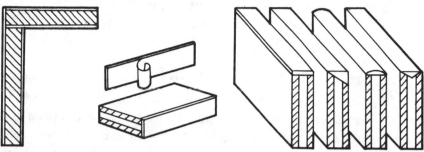

accurately, and are done only if the added width of a piece of trim is absolutely unacceptable.

If the exposed edge is the corner of a plywood box, you might rabbet one of the edges down to the back of the face veneer and overlap it across the edge of the joining piece.

JOINING   The plywood manufacturers claim you can make any joint with plywood and hold it together with glue plus nails or screws. That is true if the panel you are working with is more than ½" thick. If the wood is less than ½" thick, the edges, which have a minimum of holding power to begin with, are practically worthless. So anytime you are working with plywood that is thinner than ½", all of your joints must be supported with some kind of corner block as well as a strong glue.

When joining any man-made wood that is less than ½" thick, you will need to give the joint full support.

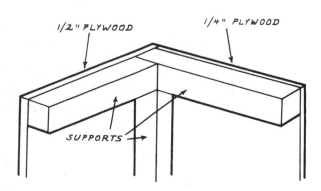

HARDBOARD

Hardboard is another man-made wood. It has in recent years gained favor among cabinetmakers as the material to use for drawer bottoms and cabinet backs. Hardwood has no grain, and is stable in that it will not shrink or swell and is equally strong in all directions. You can saw it, nail it and paint it without any trouble at all.

How Hardboard Is Sold

Hardboard is made by refining wood chips down to their fibers and then impregnating them with a chemical. This makes a goo that is then compressed and dried under intense heat until it becomes a thin, continuous sheet of wood which can be cut to any size desired. It is manufactured in thicknesses of 1/16" to 3/4" and the usual panel size is 4'×8', although you can find widths of up to 5' and lengths to 16'.

Hardboard is sold as three types: standard, tempered and service. *Standard* is high strength, water resistant and will accept any finish. *Tempered* is even harder and stronger and will accept a finish even better. *Service* is relatively soft and does not finish as well, but is excellent wherever you need a light material, such as for the back of a large shelf case.

Hardboard is also manufactured in a whole range of finishes, including embossed patterns that simulate leather, basket weave and all kinds of hardwood grains. There are also acoustical tiles made of hardboard, and perforated boards that are so widely used as pegboards. Pegboards come with evenly spaced holes in 4'×8' sheets which can hold all kinds of hooks, pegs and hangers. They are an important material to consider anytime you are constructing storage that must hang a large number of odd-sized objects such as tools.

Working with Hardboard

There is no grain to worry about, but don't expect hardboard to span large areas without giving it proper support. Support is needed anytime you are using hardboard vertically, as you would when backing a cabinet, because even the ¾"-thick versions have considerable give. If you drive a nail into the edge of any hardboard, you can assume it will not hold by itself, and neither will screws. You must deal with hardboard edges by gluing them and adding a corner block which you can attach by going through the hardboard face.

CUTTING   Hardboard can be sawed with any hand or power saw, but the chemicals used in its manufacture will dull normal blades rather quickly. It is advisable to use tungsten-carbide-tipped blades if you are using power tools.

DRILLING AND NAILING   Whenever drilling or nailing hardboard, be certain the material is *fully* supported. If you nail through the shiny side you will consistently get smooth edges in the back side, but if you go through the back side first, the face will chip at the edges. Clamping a piece of scrap against the good side may help prevent chipping.

When nailing a hardboard panel to anything, always begin at the center and work out toward the edges. Fasteners should be placed no closer than ¼" to any edge, and be no more than 4" apart. Always use glue in a joint made with hardboard; any glue can be used as long as it is applied according to the manufacturer's instructions.

BENDING   Hardboard can be bent around a solid curved frame and glue-nailed or screwed in place without cracking or breaking. Tempered hardboard will bend more readily than standard or service. If the radius is too sharp to easily make a dry bend, dampen the wood with hot water or steam.

PAINTING   Hardboard will accept almost any paint, but seal it first with a coat of shellac, enamel undercoat or primer-sealer. You can use a pad, brush, roller or spray gun to apply the paint.

PARTICLEBOARD

There are something like 20 different kinds of particleboard on the market today. Each is sold under a different commercial name and includes different chemicals in its composition. But all particleboard is essentially made up of wood chips, sawdust and a resin adhesive, and compressed into the shape of a panel under intense heat and pressure. The resulting material is heavy, equally strong in all directions, resistant and very stable. Its edges, like those of all man-made woods, have almost no holding power for either screws or nails.

Particleboard in all its forms has proven to be an ideal and inexpensive material for such items as sliding doors and counter tops. Because its cost remains considerably lower than other wood products, it is also beginning to show up as the primary material for cabinets and shelves. It is too heavy for use in large swinging doors because screws cannot hold the hinges in place; however, you can use bolts instead. If the span is supported every 2', particleboard can be used for shelving.

How Particleboard Is Sold

The premier particleboard is flakeboard, which is manufactured with a unique resin and carefully sliced pieces (flakes) of wood; these elements make it easy to work with and finish. After flakeboard there is little difference in the composition of other particleboard. Depending on its components, particleboard weighs between 30 and 50 pounds per cubic foot; flakeboard ranges between 40 and 50 pounds. The material is available in thicknesses of ¼" to 2", and comes in panels 2' to 5' wide and 4' to 16' long, with 4'×8' the most usual size available.

Working with Particleboard

Particleboard is a tough material to work. It is heavy and cumbersome, and the resin that holds it together will almost immediately dull normal saw blades and drill bits. So if you are using any power tools with particleboard, put on your tungsten-carbide bits or blades. When it is cut with a power tool, particleboard creates an extremely fine dust that lingers in the air for hours. If your workshop is not adequately ventilated and if you do not have a good waste-removal system, wear a mask.

CUTTING Particleboard can be cut with any hand or power saw, but it is a mean material to saw by hand, so whenever possible go to a power saw.

JOINING Always glue particleboard. Its edges are vulnerable to breakage and are not very strong to begin with, so use threaded or coated nails. You can nail or drill through particleboard without having it chip or break, but pulling out a nail may cause the whole area around the fastener to come off with the nail.

Provided you use carbide-tipped bits, you can rout, shape or dado particleboard with no problems. The best way of joining particleboard is with a tongue-and-groove, dowel or spline joint; rabbets and butt joints are not really adequate.

FOUR
Tools and Supplies

THE TOOLS YOU WILL NEED TO CONSTRUCT ANY storage in your home are a hammer, saw and occasionally a screwdriver. Obviously, the more sophisticated a cutting tool you have, the easier the cutting will be. Any of the woods normally used in storage construction can be cut with a hand saw. But if you intend to do very much cutting, spend the $30 for a good circular hand power saw, or at least buy a saber saw for around $20.

Just to wet your whistle, consider the outer reaches of capability of a table (bench) saw or a radial arm saw. Both of these stationary saws guarantee accurate, straight cuts through any material put before their blades, even if you have never used one before. They cut not only straight lines, but also miters, bevels, compound angles and curves. Better still, both saws permit you to dado or plough grooves in wood to hold the ends of a shelf. The radial arm saw offers even more capabilities, such as sanding, drilling and routing. If you can afford either tool and have the space to install it in your home, don't hesitate to spend $300 to buy one. Either will make you an instant professional, no matter what kind of carpentry you are doing.

If you are in the mood to get fancy, you can add to the table or radial arm saws a joiner-planer, drill press and, perhaps most important of all, a stationary disk-belt sander. The objective in cutting wood is to make a straight cut along the exact lines you have specified, and then to make certain the cut is smooth and even. A stationary power saw will get you very close the first time; a joiner-planer takes the bumps in the wood down to your guidelines. A sander smooths the evened

36.

edges until they are arrow straight and smooth. Sanding is the essence of good finishing, and a stationary power sander takes all the guesswork out of prefinishing your wood.

Most people are not wood freaks. They only want to put together efficient, useful storage at a minimum of time or money. The cheapest way toward that aim is via hand tools; the best compromise is a complement of carefully selected power and hand tools that will shorten your working time and drain the least possible amount from your budget. That combination of tools includes:

one hand circular power saw and dado blade set
one ⅜" electric drill, with bits and sanding disk
one 16-ounce claw hammer
a set of four standard-blade and one Phillips-head screwdrivers
one electric vibrating sander
one block plane
one surform tool
one utility saw with both wood and hacksaw blades
one nailset
one folding rule or metal tape
one combination square
one carpenter's level
a set of three chisels

HAND SAWS

Assuming you don't want to spring $25 for a good circular power saw, you are relegated to using hand saws. If all you are cutting is the width of pine boards or plywood in any direction, use a crosscut saw that has between 7 and 12 precision-ground teeth per inch. The fewer the teeth, the faster the saw will cut, but at the expense of leaving rough edges on the wood; the more teeth, the smoother the cut. In either case you will have to do some edge sanding.

To work with a crosscut saw, start the saw on the waste side of the cutting line (the side you intend to discard) and use the back part of the blade (nearest the handle). Draw several short strokes to embed the blade in the wood, then use your thumb as a guide and hold the blade at about a 45° angle to the wood surface. Crosscut saws cut on both the backward and forward strokes, so you do not have to apply any special pressure either way. As you come to the end of the cut, be careful to fully support both sides of the wood so that it does not splinter.

Ripsaws have between 5½ and 6½ teeth per inch and the blade is typically 26″ long. Each tooth is shaped like a tiny chisel that has its cutting edge angled across the blade. As a result, the teeth chop their way between the fibers of the wood, which makes the saw difficult to use when you want to go across the grain.

To begin a rip cut use the front of the blade, where there are 6½ teeth per inch, and pull a few short strokes to start a groove. Ripsaws cut only on the forward stroke, so it is surprising that you can slice 10′ of pine board in about a minute, if your arm doesn't fall off in the process. If the saw wanders away from your cutting line (and it will), gradually guide it back to the line; don't bend it sharply.

The cuts you make with a ripsaw are normally very long, so there are a pair of tricks to make your work easier. One of these is to jam a wedge of wood between the edges of the cut behind your saw to keep the wood apart and give the saw blade freedom to move. The second trick is to clamp or nail a strip of wood along your cutting line and keep the saw blade against it as you cut.

The cost of a good hand saw is about $12 or $15, and you will need both the crosscut saw and ripsaw. That is an outlay of between $24 and $30—the price of a good circular power saw.

CIRCULAR POWER SAWS

These are the rough carpenter's best friend because they are indispensable for on-site cutting. You can saw a 2×4 in half in about 60 seconds using a crosscut hand saw and a lot of hard labor. You can do the same job in 10 seconds using a circular power saw, with absolute accuracy and next to no effort. When it comes to cutting plywood, the circular saw is unparalleled even by the stationary saws. It will also cut miters, bevels, dadoes and rabbets, plus, with a modest amount of practice, circles. The tool is a little heavy but it rests against the wood while you are cutting. It also tends to pull itself through the wood, which leaves nothing for you to do but guide it.

The baseplate of the saw is held to the case with a wing nut which can be loosened to raise or lower the plate, and thus control the depth of your cut. It is not necessary to have any more than ¼" of the blade extending below the wood; you can also keep the blade from cutting all the way through the wood, which means you can cut dadoes, ploughs and rabbets. You can also swing the baseplate sideways so that the saw sits at an angle against the wood, allowing any degree of bevel cut.

Saw Blades

The versatility of circular power saws does not end with the saw itself. There are a variety of specialty blades available: the combination blade, which will both rip and crosscut; rip blades that are designed specifically for ripping but will cut in any direction; and plywood/veneer blades which contain upward of 200 teeth. Two hundred teeth do not cut—they nibble away at the wood and reduce the amount of chipping in the face veneers of plywood panels.

You can also buy tungsten-carbide-tipped blades which have between a dozen and 60 teeth. Each tooth is made of carbide, an unusually strong metal which holds its sharpness up to five times longer than any other metal. The carbide-tipped blades cost twice as much as other blades but they are worth the money, particularly if you have to cut a lot of particleboard or hardboard. The carbide blades are so sharp that if they have a great many tips, they will cut plywood and softwood so smooth that practically no sanding is necessary.

DADO BLADES Dado blades are the professional's secret weapon. They are actually a set of two full blades plus half a dozen chippers that are assembled on the saw arbor to create a single cutting unit which leaves a wide slot in the wood. The width of the slot can

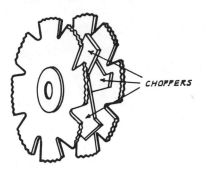

Dado blades for a hand circular saw are 3½" in diameter and cost around $15.

CHOPPERS

range from ⅛" up to almost an inch (depending on how many of the chippers you put on).

What these blades can do with a single pass of the saw is cut a dado, plough or rabbet that is exactly the width of, say, a shelf thickness. The shelf can then be glued and nailed in the slot, giving it unmatched strength as well as a professional look. A circular saw will do the same kind of routing without a dado blade, but with a lot more work on your part and considerably greater room for error.

Cutting

It is possible to develop a very steady hand with circular saws so that eventually you may need nothing more than a line drawn on the wood to guide your cutting. But a more reliable method is to clamp a straight board or metal edge of some sort along your cut line and keep the side of the saw's baseplate tightly against it while cutting. This is particularly true when you are making the first two or three cuts in a plywood panel where you may have as much as 8' of wood to go through and don't want to make any mistakes.

SABER SAWS

The power alternative to the circular saw is a saber saw. It is light, portable and specifically designed to cut curves in almost any material, provided you insert the right blade in its chuck. You can purchase a very serviceable saber saw for less than $20 and a complete complement of blades for about $3. The blades look like serrated knives and have varying widths, lengths, strengths and numbers of teeth.

Because the machine is so light, it will tend to wander away from your cutting line, so it is always preferable to clamp a guide to the stock you are cutting. You can really learn about saber saws only by using one. The base should be held firmly against the wood (even though it tends to rise up at one end or the other), because the blades are so narrow you must guide the saw more slowly than you do a circular saw. Don't be surprised if you break a lot of blades; even the old hands will inadvertently twist the machine and snap a blade. Just be sure that you buy a model that will accommodate one of the replacement blades sold at most hardware stores. A full set of saber-saw blades consists of perhaps seven or eight different blades, each with a special purpose. Together they allow you to cut all kinds of wood and metal, leather, paper, cardboard, plastics and practically any other material. You can even buy tungsten-carbide blades for a saber saw.

There are two ways of starting a cut in the middle of a board. You can drill a hole in the scrap area that is large enough to accommodate the blade and then saw out to your cutting line. Or you can start with a plunge cut. The plunge cut is begun by tipping the saw forward on its baseplate until the tip of the blade just touches the wood. Then the saw is turned on and the machine is slowly tipped back as the blade digs into the wood. When the blade is all the way through the material and the saw is upright, begin cutting along your guideline.

ELECTRIC DRILLS

Hand-drilling holes is hard work. Don't do it. The time and energy you can save with a power drill is worth infinitely more than the $15 or $20 you have to lay out for the tool. Electric drills are virtually an entire shop in themselves, and if you spend a little more to get a variable-speed $3/8$"-chuck machine, you can collect a retinue of accessories that will let you drill, sand, scrape paint, saw, rout, shape, grind, buff, drive and remove screws, drill holes around a corner and even pump water.

Like the saber saw, the power drill requires the right bit for the job at hand. Bits range from $1/64''$ to $2''$ in diameter, or you can use a hole saw, which lets you drill holes as large as $6''$. The bits used for drilling wood are made of strong steel that will go through most woods, but if you are up against metal, use a high-speed bit made of specially tempered steel. Masonry requires a carbide-tipped masonry bit. Many drills are sold with a starter set of bits and a sanding-wheel attachment. The wheel permits you to use a sanding disk, which is excellent for evening off lumps in the edges of wood where you drifted away from the cutting line.

Drills are designated by their chuck size—$1/2''$, $3/8''$ or $1/4''$. Actually, the size of the chuck is not as important as the power of the machine and its versatility. A variable-speed machine has a switch that allows you to speed up or slow down the bit's number of revolutions per second, which is useful when you are going through metal or other tough material. Some of the many accessories also require a different driving speed from the one used just for drilling. If the tool has a reversing action, it can rotate the bit backward (counterclockwise), so pulling the bit out of the material is easier. You can also insert a screwdriver blade in the chuck and either tighten or loosen screws, a handy capability if you are attaching a 6'-long piano hinge to a storage cabinet and have to put in 144 screws.

VIBRATING SANDERS

You can build storage without owning a vibrating sander, but the advantage of having one is that you can cover large areas quickly without doing any more than steering the machine over the wood. The circular sanding operation needed to remove bumps leaves round scratches in the surface of the wood, which will surely stand out under a clear finish such as varnish, and may even appear through paint. The vibrator will sand away those scratches if it is guided in the direction of the wood grain. Vibrating sanders cost about $15 and are worth the money if you intend to do a lot of finished cabinetwork. Alternatively, you can purchase a vibrating attachment for your electric drill for about $5.

SURFORM TOOLS

The surform tool, no matter what it looks like, is a handle that has a metal "cheese grater" attached to its bottom. These tools are new to the market but are now widely sold because they are an effective way of evening out a piece of wood and are especially good on end grains and plywood edges. In fact, they are the safest tools to use on plywood because they tend to chip the face veneers less than any other implement. The tiny, sharpened holes in the grater are sharp and tough enough to shave metals; when they finally become dull you can replace them for about a dollar.

Surform tools can be fitted with different "cheese grater" grades. The design of the tool itself has no bearing on its effectiveness.

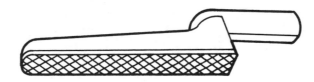

PLANES

The smallest, most versatile hand plane is the block plane, which is about 7" long and fits easily in the palm of your hand. Planing is the quickest, most controlled way of reducing the edge or roughness in a board. It is certainly faster than sanding and yet will take off less wood than a saw. Planes all have adjustable, removable blades that are held in place through a slot in the bottom of the tool with a knob or lever. The blade should be set to peel off large amounts of material until you get close to the end of the job. Then reset the blade so that your cuts are shallower. The blade should always be sharp; you can remove it from the plane and hone it the same way you would a carving knife.

Anytime you are planing the edges of wood, particularly plywood, work with the grain; start with the tool flat against the wood and apply a steady, even pressure as you push forward. As long as you are going with the grain you can keep pushing until you run out of wood.

When you plane the end grain of a board, the plane will tend to leave a rough surface that must be sanded afterward, and you can expect to have splintered edges no matter how careful you are. Work from the edges of an end grain toward the center of the wood, using short strokes. After you have trimmed the sides down to the desired line, you will have a hump in the middle of the wood which can be planed level without further chipping the edges.

Beyond the tools described here you will need at various times a carpenter's hammer, preferably with a 16-ounce head; both standard-blade and Phillips-head screwdrivers; either a folding rule or metal measuring tape; a level; and a combination square. The level and combination square are particularly important for getting work square and for making sure shelves are not so crooked that things can roll off them.

*Eight ways of using a combination
square.*

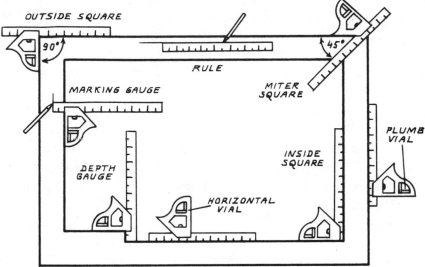

FASTENERS AND ADHESIVES

Most storage is assembled with nails and, if the builder is wise, glue. Occasionally a screw is necessary for added strength or if the piece is to be highly visible; bolts are an alternative fastener used in large, heavy units that may have to be disassembled sometime.

Nails

You might think that there is nothing complicated about driving nails into wood. You pick up your hammer, tap the head of the nail a few times until it can stand up by itself, remove your fingers from the general area and whack away. That is more or less true, except you have to bear some things in mind about the type of wood you are nailing and its ability to hold the nail in place.

SELECTING THE RIGHT NAIL Nails come in all sizes and shapes and you could use almost any of them in a storage project.

Basically, you should reach for a common nail (one with a large head) unless you are nailing into a surface that will be seen. Then you use a finishing nail, which has a very small head that can be driven below the surface of the wood and covered with wood putty or plastic wood.

Sometimes the corrugated nail is useful, particularly for a butt joint where two surfaces meet too far away from the edges of the wood to allow nails to be driven into the joint. An example of this would be two 9"-wide boards placed at a right angle to each other to form a corner shelf. You cannot buy a nail 9" or 10" long, so you would drive corrugated nails across the joint to hold the two boards together.

You might use a spiral or threaded nail in many situations. These have screw-type threads in their shanks for better gripping. They are ideal when you are nailing to an end grain, or to plywood or any of the man-made woods.

Nails keep pieces of wood together because when they are driven between the fibers of the wood the fibers spring away from the metal shank and then snap back against it. The more nail surface you have, the better the nail will hold, and you can increase nail surface by using longer or fatter nails. However, there is a point at which a fat nail will split the wood, and there are times when a thin, pointed nail will do the same. There are three guidelines to follow when selecting the proper nail for the wood you are assembling:

1. The length of nail should be less than three times the thickness of the first piece of wood it enters. Thus, if you are nailing a ¾"-thick board, the nail should be less than 2¼" long.

2. When nailing together pieces of wood of different thicknesses, the nail should be long enough to pass through the thinner piece and go no more than two-thirds of the way through the thicker piece. If you were nailing a 1" board to a 3" board, your nail would be only 3" long.

3. When nailing into the end of a board, use a spiral or threaded nail whenever possible. The threaded nails must be hammered a little more slowly than regular nails so that their threads have a chance to grip the wood, but they are a lot harder to pull out.

Nails used in storage-making.

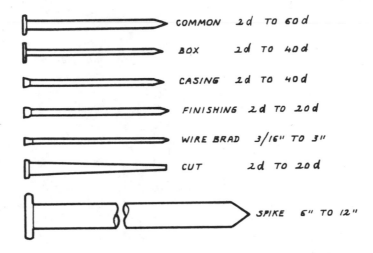

COMMON   2d TO 60 d

BOX   2d TO 40 d

CASING   2d TO 40 d

FINISHING 2d TO 20 d

WIRE BRAD 3/16" TO 3"

CUT   2d TO 20 d

SPIKE   6" TO 12"

DRIVING NAILS   Whenever possible, drive your nails at an angle and, when placing more than one nail in a board, set each one at a different angle. This is particularly important when you are going into an end grain.

If you put a nail into the end of a board it will go between the fibers of the wood very easily. It will come out just as easily. So your objective is to get the nail to go across the fibers rather than between them.

You also want to position the nail so that any load it must bear will be on top of its head, which will tend to drive the nail deeper into the wood. Similarly, if the load is bearing down on the nail point, it will eventually push the nail out of the wood.

The second most reliable way to position a nail is to drive it in so that the load will push against its shank. Consider, though, that if you nail a shelf between two uprights and drive two nails into each end of the board, the only thing holding the 25 pounds of books you put on that shelf is four little pieces of metal. Sooner or later the shelf will collapse, because either the nails bend or the wood splits at the board ends around them. In any situation where you cannot get most of the load across at least part of the shank of the nail, find another way of fastening—with an angle iron, a cleat, straps, bolts or screws.

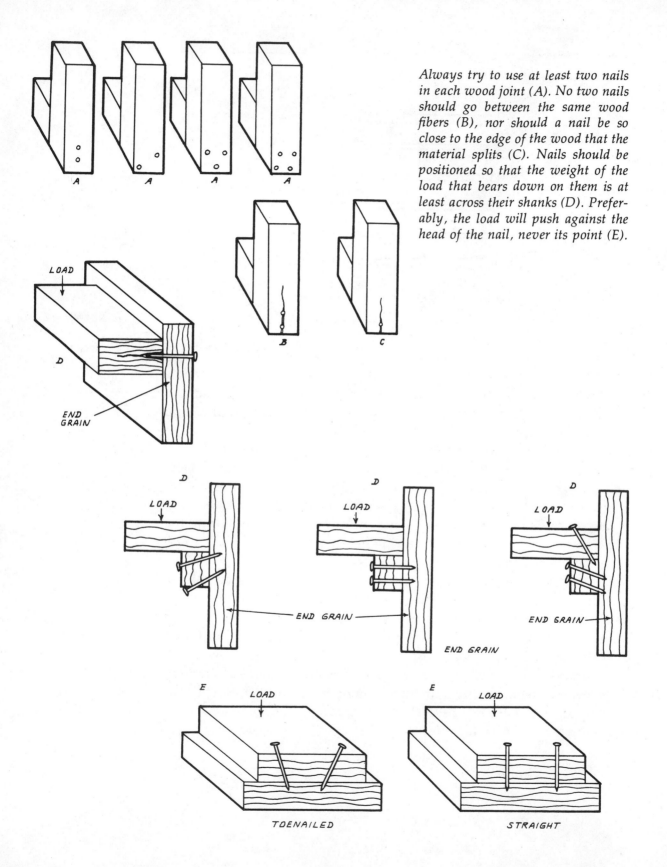

Always try to use at least two nails in each wood joint (A). No two nails should go between the same wood fibers (B), nor should a nail be so close to the edge of the wood that the material splits (C). Nails should be positioned so that the weight of the load that bears down on them is at least across their shanks (D). Preferably, the load will push against the head of the nail, never its point (E).

Screws

Screws are manufactured from steel, copper, brass and bronze, and have a rather cumbersome system of designation. The diameter of the shank has a number from 2 to 24, which does not relate to a specific shank diameter. When buying screws you must give this number plus the length you desire. Every number comes in a full range of lengths that are proportionate to the shank diameter. You will not find a #2 screw much longer than ½", but the #24s go up to 6". Somewhere there is a screw diameter and length to suit each of your needs.

There are three kinds of screw heads: flat, oval and round. The flathead screws have bevels under their heads so that you can countersink them in wood and then cover them over with a wood filler. The length of a flathead screw is measured from the top of its head to the tip of its point. Roundhead screws have a rounded top to their heads but are flat on the shank side. They are not meant to be hidden in the wood and are measured from their point to the underside of the head. Screws with oval heads are a combination of the flathead and roundhead types—the underside of their heads is beveled and the top is rounded. You can countersink them, and their lengths are figured from their points to the center of their heads.

The three types of screw heads, and how screw lengths are measured.

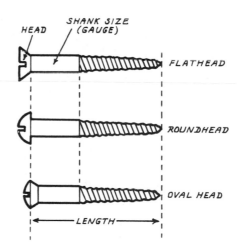

SELECTING THE RIGHT SCREW The screw you use depends on whether you want the head to show or not. If you don't care whether the head is seen or if the screw is to act as a decorative feature, you can use either an oval or roundhead screw. If you want to hide the screw, buy flatheads and countersink them.

Next, consider the wood you are working with. If you are going into hardwood you can use a thinner screw than you can with softwoods. But as a rule of thumb, always reach for the fattest screw you can get away with that won't split the wood. As for its length, make sure that it is at least ⅛″ less than the combined thicknesses of the pieces you are attaching. When you are working with plywood you have less leeway in your choice of screws. Plywood manufacturers are very specific about the correct screw size for different thicknesses of plywood, to minimize the chance of splintering the face veneers.

Plywood Thickness	Screw Size	Screw Length
¾″ to 1″	#8	1½″
⅝″	#8	1¼″
½″	#6	1¼″
⅜″	#6	1″
¼″	#4	1″

Most screws have a single slot cut across their heads which will accept the blade of a standard screwdriver. The slots vary in width, as do the widths and thicknesses of screwdriver blades. You can also buy all screw sizes with Phillips-head slots. These are two cuts that form a cross in the flat top of the head and require a Phillips-head screwdriver, which contains an X-shaped point at the end of its blade. The advantage of Phillips-head screws is simply that the screwdriver tends to slip off the head less often and mar the surfaces around the screw. Some people also say that the Phillips head gives you a better purchase on the screw so it can be driven more quickly.

No matter what the screw head looks like, all screws perform the same service with the same strength; not only do they hold two pieces of wood, they also tend to draw them tightly together, locking them in place.

PILOT HOLES AND COUNTERSINKS   The threads are the only parts of a screw that actually grip the wood. The metal in between the threads that forms the screw shank has no bearing on joining the wood. But just turning a screw into softwood takes considerable effort; it is almost impossible to do with hardwoods. So people normally drill pilot holes for their screws. The pilot hole should be no larger than the diameter of the screw shank, or the threads will have nothing to bite into. When choosing a drill bit to make any pilot hole, hold the screw up to the light and match the bit against the threaded part of the screw. If you can see just the threads above and below the bit, the bit is the correct diameter. If you cannot see the threads, get a smaller-diameter bit.

If you intend to countersink a screw, first drill the pilot hole. Then select a bit that is the same diameter as the screw head and drill a fraction of an inch into the pilot hole. Be careful to go only deep enough to bring the head of the screw just below the surface of the wood, so it can be covered with wood filler.

If a bit is placed in front of the threads of a screw and the threads can be seen above and below it, the bit is the proper diameter for making a pilot hole.

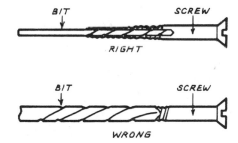

DRIVING AND REMOVING SCREWS   To drive a screw, select a screwdriver blade that fits snugly into the slot of the screw and is no wider than the screw head. If the blade is loose in the slot, it will slip endlessly and chew up the slot until you can no longer get a purchase. If the blade is too large for the screw slot you will not be able to turn the screw at all.

If you damage a screw slot it is possible to clean it with a small metal file or deepen it with a hacksaw blade, but in most cases it is easier to discard the screw and start all over again.

You may have heard that you can rub soap between the threads of a screw and it will go into the wood more easily. That is true, but over the years the soap will harden and act like an adhesive, literally gluing the screw in place. If you think you might ever want to remove the screw, use candle wax or graphite instead of soap. Never use oil—it will stain the wood and the stain will show through any finish you attempt to put over it.

There are two ways of removing a stubborn screw, short of cutting it with a hacksaw. Try tightening the screw (turning it clockwise), then twisting it counterclockwise. Tighten and loosen the screw repeatedly until it comes free. If that fails, hold the tip of a hot iron against the head of the screw until it becomes warm. Then remove the iron and wait for the screw to cool before trying to unscrew it. Heat expands the metal and, as it cools again, the screw should break loose from whatever is holding it.

Bolts

Bolts are really heavy-duty screws. They can be found in all diameters and in lengths from ¼″ to 16″ with square, round or hexagonal heads.

Carriage bolts have squared-off threaded ends that accept a nut which is tightened on the shaft with a wrench or pliers.

Lag bolts have pointed threads and hexagonal or square heads. You can drill pilot holes for them but they are threaded into the wood using a wrench or pliers. Lag bolts are a strong support for any cabinet or shelf attached to a wall, provided you have a stud to screw them into.

The hanger bolt is threaded to accept a bolt at one end and has a pointed thread at the other. You can screw the pointed end into a wall stud and then bolt a cabinet to the hanger. The cabinet will probably never come down. (See illustrations of other types of bolts.)

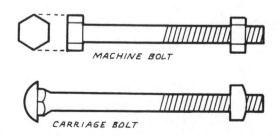

MACHINE BOLT

CARRIAGE BOLT

Machine, carriage, lag and hanger bolts.

LAG BOLT

HANGER BOLT

Anchors

There are several devices for anchoring storage to a wall; the one you use depends on the wall's composition. If you are up against a brick or cement wall, you can use either flat masonry nails or a knurled-thread nail. The knurled thread has nearly straight flutes along its shank which can grip the masonry and hold considerable weight.

Another way of anchoring in masonry or plaster walls is to use a carbide-tipped masonry bit and drill a hole just large enough for a lead, fiber or plastic plug. The plug is inserted in the hole and an accompanying screw is threaded into it. The screw is too big for the plug and purposely splits it, forcing the plug to grip the concrete or brick around it. Lead plugs are particularly effective, although all of them work well.

For hollow walls—those made with drywall panels—there are a variety of toggle bolts and mollys. Again, you must drill a hole large enough for the anchor, then insert it and turn the bolt that comes with it. The unit will flare out behind the wallboard and lock the bolt in place so that it will hold whatever it is you wish to hang from it.

Basic types of wall anchors.

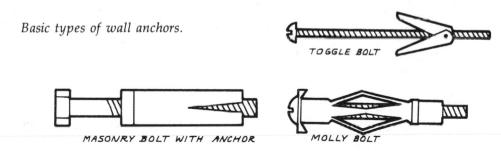

TOGGLE BOLT

MASONRY BOLT WITH ANCHOR

MOLLY BOLT

Adhesives

There are dozens of adhesives on the market today, and all of them are better than the glues of times past. But each is made for a special purpose such as gluing wood or plastic or metal, and only a few can handle all materials. In constructing storage, you should not have to do too much intricate gluing and clamping, though some wood glues must be clamped for as long as 24 hours.

Most of your storage-making needs will involve applying glue to joints which are also held together with nails or screws, and as soon as a fastener is driven into the joint it is automatically clamped anyway. The major reason for using glue in all joints is that wood tends to "breathe" with changes of weather. It swells and shrinks when the humidity changes, and every time this happens the metal fasteners become a little looser. A glued joint is more stable; the wood is forced to expand in other directions so that the fasteners are not disturbed as much.

You can use any of the white (liquid resin) or cream-colored (aliphatic) glues in wooden joints; they will both withstand upwards of 3,000 pounds per square inch (psi) of pressure. They are easy to squeeze out of their plastic bottles, too.

If you want a really powerful glue, one that does not require any fasteners, the acrylics deliver up to 6,000 psi and will set in as little as five minutes. Then there are the epoxies and the resorcinols, all of which can deliver more than ample strength to any joint if you apply them exactly according to the manufacturer's instructions.

NOTE: *Don't try to use a modern glue in any way other than that specified by the instructions, or it won't work.*

ABRASIVES

All abrasives used to be called sandpaper but these days there is never any sand in them. Modern abrasives are made in sheets, rolls, belts and disks which can be used on a number of different sanding machines. The sheets are most often 9"×11" and are used for hand sanding. The rolls fit on both drum and spindle sanders; the belts come in different lengths and widths to fit the various belt sanders on the market. The disks are sold in diameters of 7" to 9½" and fit on both portable and stationary sanders.

The grains you see on a piece of abrasive are in fact tiny individual cutting tools much like chisels or saw teeth. They are made of flint, garnet, aluminum oxide or silicon carbide, and are glued to some kind of paper or cloth backing to make up the abrasive.

There are two kinds of abrasives: open and closed grain. The open grain has spaces on its backing between the pieces of abrasive that are comparatively large and coarse. Open-grain abrasives are used for rough smoothing and evening. The closed-grain abrasives have smaller pieces of abrasive very close together and are used for smoothing wood.

Grits

All four abrasive materials can be purchased in a range of grits from very fine (superfine) to very coarse. Which of the four you use does not really matter, although garnet and silicon carbide are considered best for work on the softwoods normally used in storage making. But the abrasive you use is not half as important as how you use it.

The Only Way to Sand

No matter what you have been told about sanding, there is only one way of smoothing wood. If you neglect any of the four steps involved, the finish you apply to the wood will be less than it should be.

1. *Roughing.* Begin with a coarse or very coarse grit, whichever is just rough enough to even the surface of the wood and get rid of any excessive roughness. A circular or disk sander can be used only at this stage.

2. *Blending.* Using a medium grit, you'll achieve a fairly smooth surface if you do your sanding long enough. You can put medium grits on a vibrating or belt sander.

3. *Fine sanding.* Go to the fine grits, which will get rid of the tiny scratches left by a circular or belt sander. If you are planning on applying a clear finish, go through this stage by hand; otherwise a vibrating sander will do a creditable job.

4. *Finishing.* The only way to do this is with very fine or

superfine grits applied with the grain, by hand. You are now removing or blending all scratches.

If you are sanding shelves that are to be painted, it is usually acceptable to skip the finish stage, but let your conscience be your guide. Anytime you intend to apply a clear finish (varnish or shellac), get rid of all the scratches or they will stand out with glaring clarity.

It is possible to begin sanding with the medium grits. Plywood, for example, usually is smooth enough so that no roughing is necessary.

HINTS FOR HAND SANDING   Sooner or later you have to put away your sanding machines and "lay hands" on the wood. When you do, here are some things to remember:

1. Hand sanding is usually done with garnet paper.

2. Always wrap the abrasive around a block of wood, rather than folding it into a pad. You will have a tendency to inadvertently round off corners and edges unless the abrasive is stiffly supported.

3. Always sand with the grain of the wood, no matter which way the grain is going.

4. This is not easy to do, but try to keep a constant pressure on the surface, just enough so that the abrasive barely cuts into the surface of the wood.

5. Clean the abrasive often with a stiff brush so that the grit does not become clogged—you'll waste a lot of energy otherwise.

6. When sanding an outside corner or edge, curve or "break" it just enough to prevent splintering and make it feel smooth.

7. Sanding will be a lot easier if you do all the rough and medium and some of the fine work *before* you put together your project. It is particularly hard to get at assembled shelves while maintaining even pressure on the abrasive. The undersides of high shelves, by the way, are usually visible, so they should be properly finished.

WOOD FILLERS

There are several types of wood fillers on sale at most hardware stores. Some of them come in cans and are the consistency of putty; others are a powder that must be mixed with water until they thicken enough to be applied to wood. All are intended for filling cracks, splits, gouges and minor imperfections in wood, and can also be used to fill in holes above countersunk screws or nails. All of them work well. They require drying time, which may be as short as a few minutes or as long as overnight, but when they are hard you can plane, sand, saw, drill, paint or varnish them.

Don't be surprised if one application of a wood filler is not enough. The material shrinks as it dries and sometimes leaves cracks, or will settle in the middle of a hole and leave a dent. When the first application is dry, simply cover it with more filler, mounding the material a fraction of an inch above the surface of the wood. Even the mound may sink slightly, but you should have enough left to sand down until it forms a smooth surface continuous with the wood.

FIVE

Storage Assembly

NO MATTER WHAT THE STORAGE PROJECT, THERE IS a specific order of construction to follow. You don't have to memorize it; most likely you will do it automatically. However, it is useful to have a general idea of where you are going and how you will get there. The procedure divides into three major stages, each of which contains several steps.

I. *PLANNING*
1. Identify your specific storage needs—what objects must be stored.
2. Decide on the kind of storage necessary—shelves, cabinets, etc.
3. Choose a final look for the project. Will it resemble other units in the room or have a unique appearance?
4. Sketch the project, including all dimensions.
5. Make up a Bill of Materials (see page 22) and make the necessary purchases; be certain all the tools you need are on hand.

II. *CONSTRUCTION*
1. Measure and mark all material for cutting.
2. Cut all plywood and solid stock.
3. Make all joints—dadoes, miters, rabbets, etc.
4. Fill all imperfections with wood filler. Rough- and medium-sand all parts.
5. Cut and put together all subassemblies—drawers, doors and their frames.
6. Assemble all pieces.

III. *FINISHING*
  1. Complete all fine and finish sanding.
  2. Add molding and trim.
  3. Apply undercoat or primer; sand when dry.
  4. Apply final coats, sanding between each application.
  5. Oil-rub or polish the final coat.
  6. Attach all hardware.

PLANNING

The sketches you draw should be as accurate as you can make them, not so much in terms of how straight your lines are, but in the dimensions you specify. Measure and remeasure; then measure again. The key to any woodworking project is accuracy and precision. If you cut a board ¾" too long, you can reduce it; but cut it ¾" too short, and your only recourse may be to waste the wood and start all over again with new stock. Even when you are certain that all the dimensions are absolutely accurate, keep checking as you cut and assemble the project to make sure you have not made any mistakes or that you don't run into a surprise that changes your measurements.

CONSTRUCTION

Measuring and Marking Stock

The first step in the construction phase of your project is to measure and mark all stock; you must now transfer the dimensions on your sketch to the real wood. Again, measure the wood carefully, and then put a pencil mark on it where you wish to cut. Use your combination square or some other straightedge to draw the cutting line. That line now becomes your immutable law. Your saw blade must adhere to it as nearly as possible. When you are finished cutting, half the width of the line should be just visible along the cut edge and should touch the edge at every point. If your line falls inside the edge, plane, file or sand the wood down to meet it. If the line disappears off the edge, you have a dip in the wood that is difficult to correct. This may not be too critical in, for example, the ends of a shelf. But for highly visible surfaces, try to fill the gap with wood chips, plastic wood or wood putty, or plane the entire cutting edge down to its lowest point. No matter what you do to correct it, you are in for some extra work that could have been avoided if you had been a little more careful as you sawed the piece.

SAW KERF There is one important fact which must never be forgotten: the blade of your saw is between $1/16''$ and $1/8''$ thick. If you are lopping off a couple of inches of board end, you should see your cutting line on the usable side of the wood. But if you are cutting a board into, say, three parts and you mark off all three pieces at the same time, leave at least $1/8''$ of space between the pieces. If you don't, only the first piece will be the exact length you want it to be—the others will be $1/8''$ short. Don't kid yourself—$1/8''$ can make a lot of difference when you are trying to make an absolutely square box and half the pieces are too short.

Leaving space for your saw kerf (thickness of the blade) really becomes critical when you start biting into a plywood panel. Professionals have found that it is more efficient to mark all the cutting lines on a plywood panel before they start sawing. This is a good practice because you may find that your computations were off and you actually need another inch or two of plywood. You cannot buy $1/2''$ of plywood, so the only thing to do is adjust your dimensions—before you start cutting.

As you mark off the panel (or any stock), always allow for that $1/8''$ between cuts. You can get a surprising number of pieces out of a panel

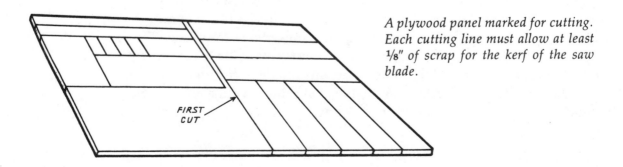

FIRST CUT

A plywood panel marked for cutting. Each cutting line must allow at least $1/8''$ of scrap for the kerf of the saw blade.

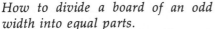

How to divide a board of an odd
width into equal parts.

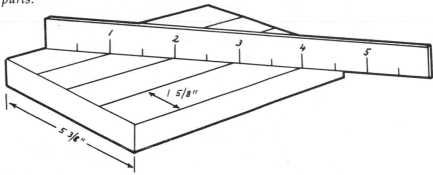

if you plan your cutting carefully. One of the best ways to plan your cuts is to use a pad of graph paper, which automatically gives you a scale to work with. Keep adjusting dimensions until you can get the most pieces possible with the least amount of waste. When you are satisfied that you are getting maximum use out of the panel, transfer your measurements to the wood itself. No matter what kind of saw you are using, a standard 4'×8' panel is cumbersome; nibbling away at its edges doesn't make it any less so. As you plan your cuts, try to allow for one or two initial long cuts that will divide it in half or in quarters, which are infinitely more manageable sizes to work with. **And never forget to allow for the thickness of your saw blade.**

QUICK TIPS FOR MEASURING You have a board 5³⁄₈" wide which you want to divide into four equal strips. Quick! How wide will each strip be? You can reach for a calculator or a pair of dividers, but it is easier to lay a ruler diagonally across the board. Place the 0 end of the ruler against one edge, and angle the ruler until the 8 touches the opposite edge. You do not have to choose 8—use any number that is evenly divisible by the number of parts you want to cut the board into. Since you want this particular board in four parts, mark off the ruler by placing a dot in the wood at the 2, 4 and 6 marks. Now measure the distance from each dot to one edge of the board. You will get 1³⁄₈", 2³⁄₄" and 4¹⁄₈". Each strip will be 1³⁄₈" wide, less one-half the width of your saw kerf, about ¹⁄₁₆". When measuring, make sure the ruler does not form a right angle across the wood—it must be placed at any other angle. Remember to choose a number that is equally divisible by the number of times you wish to divide the wood.

Suppose you are following a set of plans telling you to round off the corner of a shelf using a 2″ radius. Mark off the radius (2″) along both edges from the corner. Using your combination square, draw perpendicular lines down from the marks until they intersect. The point where the lines cross is the center of your circle. Open your compass to a radius of 2″, put the point at the intersection and draw on arc around the corner. You can plane, file, sand or saw the corner down to meet your line.

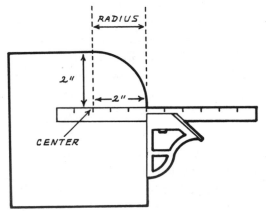

Finding the center of a curved corner.

Should you want to cut an ellipse out of the center of a piece of plywood—perhaps to hold a bathroom sink or make a tabletop—avoid the trouble of trying to work out your ellipse with just a compass and a French curve. Instead, try the procedure diagrammed here:

1. Draw two lines that cross each other at right angles at their center points. The longer line (AB) is the major axis. The shorter line (CD) is the minor axis. Open a compass or pair of dividers to a width of one-half the longer line.

2. Using one end of the minor axis as your center point (C), inscribe intersecting arcs on each side of the center of the major

The three steps in making an ellipse.

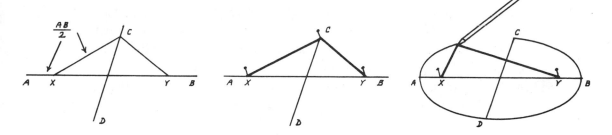

axis. Stick a pin into the crossover point in each arc (X, Y) and a third pin at the center point. Tie a string tightly around the pins so that it forms a triangle.

3. Remove the pin in the minor axis, and hold a pencil in its place so that the string is still taut. Pull the pencil all the way around the major and minor axes, always keeping the string as taut as you can. By the time your pencil is back to its starting point, you will have drawn a perfect ellipse.

Cutting

Your initial cutting is the second most important act you will perform during the construction of any project. Do it slowly and carefully, and try to make all of your mistakes on the scrap side of your cutting lines. If you are hand sawing, keep your thumb against the saw blade to help guide it along the line. If you are using a hand power saw, take time to clamp or tack a guide along the cutting line.

The guide can be any piece of straight wood—but remember that wood bends. If you are ripping the length of a plywood panel and clamp an 8' piece of 1"×2" stock along the cutting line, a clamp at each end is not enough. You must also clamp or nail the guide at least in the middle, if not at two or three points along its length, because as you press against it with the base of your saw, you will tend to bow it away from the cut line. You can even bend an 8' piece of oak, so don't be fooled by a guide that happens to be hardwood. If you are fortunate enough to be cutting with a stationary saw, your guideline can be just a pencil tick at the edge of the wood. But triple-measure your fence setting (table saw) or arm position (radial arm saw).

With stationary tools you are always better off setting a jig if you need to cut a lot of duplicate parts. It seems silly to spend time measuring and remeasuring, clamping a guide in place, testing it to be sure the saw blade will go where you want it to, and then taking 10 seconds to make your cut. But one tiny error in any cut, and your entire project may have a flaw you cannot correct or hide. **Never forget the thickness of your saw blade!**

Making Joints

Joinery is the backbone of any storage. A proper wood joint is one in which all parts of both wood surfaces meet and are securely held together. Considering how easy it is to overshoot a cutting line, it is no mean feat to achieve two straight surfaces that touch at all points—unless you use a dado blade, preferably one that is attached to a stationary saw. However, you can come close to perfection if you are willing to work your joints carefully.

The purpose of making joints is to provide extra wood surfaces that can come together and help stabilize the entire unit, thus ensuring longer durability of the project. All of the matching surfaces should, of course, be coated with a strong glue as well as nailed or screwed together.

For the record, there are a total of 10 basic woodworking joints that can be made with roughly 100 variations. The 10 joints are: butt, miter, dado, spline, rabbet, lap, tongue and groove, mortise and tenon, dowel, and dovetail. While you occasionally might want to go to any one of the 10 or its variations, for most storage only the dado, rabbet, lap and butt are ever necessary.

BUTT   The butt joint is a two-surface union most often used to form a corner. Anytime you bring two pieces of wood together, you have a butt joint. The pieces can be side by side, form a right angle or be end to end. If you happen to be joining the planed edges of two boards fresh from the lumberyard, they will probably be smooth and

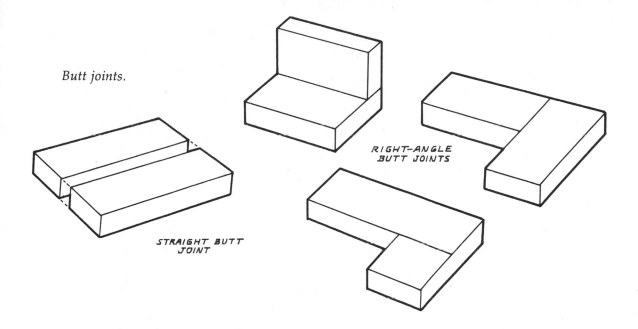

Butt joints.

RIGHT—ANGLE
BUTT JOINTS

STRAIGHT BUTT
JOINT

even enough to fit together pretty well. You can simply run a line of glue down both of the board sides and drive nails into the joint.

The trouble with butt joints is that they are inherently weak. They can wobble because they involve only two surfaces meeting, and in some instances, if the unit is to be stable, the butt joint must be held in place with a glue block in its corner or should be backed by some other material.

MITER   The decorative version of a butt joint is the miter, which is made by cutting the matching edges at any angle other than 90°; traditionally the angle is 45°. Mitering is a pretty way of joining two pieces of wood and is often used at the corners of molding or the face frame of a cabinet. If you are constructing a frame with precisely mitered corners, you will actually have a stronger unit than if you had used straight butt joints. There are two reasons for the added strength: the four angled corners exert pressure on each other, and the joints provide more bonding surfaces because they are longer than the width of the wood. Even so, the miter joint is weak. It should have a nail or two driven into its corners, and the whole mitered frame should be attached to, say, the front edges of a cabinet to really keep the joints together.

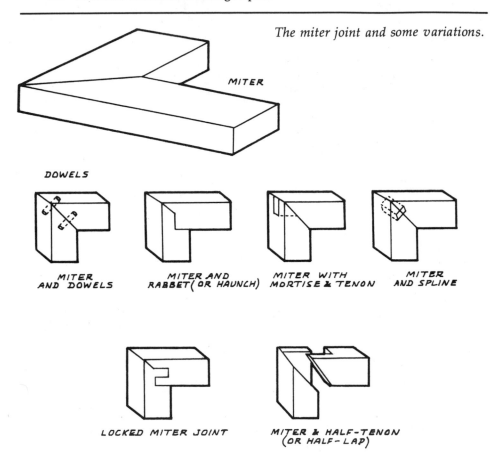

The miter joint and some variations.

MITER

DOWELS

MITER
AND DOWELS

MITER AND
RABBET(OR HAUNCH)

MITER WITH
MORTISE & TENON

MITER
AND SPLINE

LOCKED MITER JOINT

MITER & HALF-TENON
(OR HALF-LAP)

DADOES AND PLOUGHS   A dado is a slot cut across the grain of one piece of wood which can accept and hold a second piece entering it at a right angle. A plough is a long dado that runs the length of the wood, normally with the grain. Dadoes are most commonly used for assembling horizontals between vertical members. It is possible (though not preferable) to dado two verticals and shove a series of shelves into them, then stand the finished piece up without nailing, gluing or in any other way fastening the wood together.

The dado or plough should be only as wide as the thickness of the wood it must hold and should be no deeper than one-half the thick-

Different kinds of dado joints.

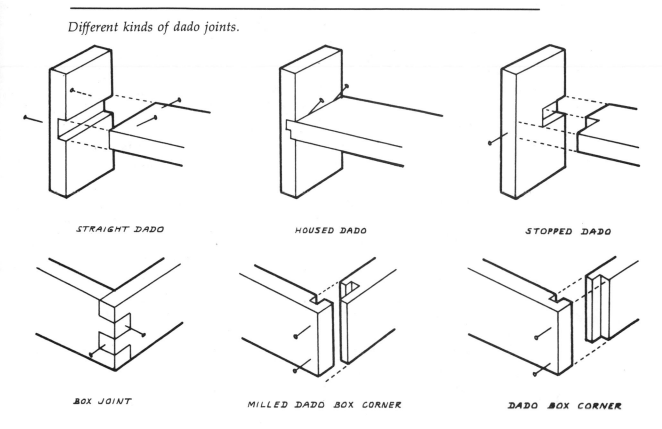

STRAIGHT DADO   HOUSED DADO   STOPPED DADO

BOX JOINT   MILLED DADO BOX CORNER   DADO BOX CORNER

ness of the wood in which it is cut. The easiest way of making any dado is to use a dado blade attached to either a stationary saw or a portable circular saw. The blade is set for the proper width and depth and then run between two parallel cutting lines. With a stationary saw you need not draw the lines—just mark their position. With a hand circular saw, you are safer with both lines to go between.

If you do not have a dado blade, you can make dadoes with a standard blade and a circular power saw. Set the saw guide so that you can cut along the inside of each of the lines. When you have made both outside cuts to the proper depth, run the saw freehand between the lines until you have cut out all of the waste material. For a ¾"-wide dado, you will need about four passes of the saw. You can also use a chisel to chop out the waste material.

If you are making the dado with a hand saw, cut the two lines to the proper depth, keeping the saw absolutely parallel to the wood so that one end of the slot is not deeper than the other. Then chisel out the waste and sand the bottom of the dado smooth.

Both the dado and plough present three gluing surfaces and lock the inserted member in place, helping to form a right angle and square the entire project. If the dadoes are snug enough and the glue you use is a strong woodworking glue (resorcinol or epoxy), you really do not need any metal fasteners. If you want to use fasteners, you can bang nails into the end grain through the back of the dado. Better still, angle some nails down through the top of the horizontal into the vertical member.

RABBET   A rabbet is really two-thirds of a dado; it is a dado that fell off the edge of the wood. Rabbets are used to form stable corners between the top, bottom and sides of a box or cabinet, and are easiest to make using a dado blade. They should be as wide as the thickness of the wood that fits into them and one-half the thickness of the wood you are joining to, but they can be any depth. If you are rabbeting two pieces of solid stock, you can rabbet one or both members. If you rabbet both pieces, you have three gluing surfaces; otherwise you have only two.

One way to hide unsightly plywood edges is to cut a rabbet in one of the pieces, going all the way to the back of the face veneer. The face veneer can then extend over the end grain of the connecting piece. Rabbets should be nailed through either of their outside surfaces, since they are essentially an open joint and do not hold the wood in place the way a dado can.

If you wish to make a rabbet with a standard saw blade on your circular power saw, cut along the guideline to the proper depth and then rout out the waste freehand with several passes of the saw. Or, after cutting along the guideline, stand the board on edge and clamp a piece of 2"×4" scrap to the back of the board. Align the scrap with the edge of the board to give your saw a stable platform to rest on. Draw a

The two rabbet joints.

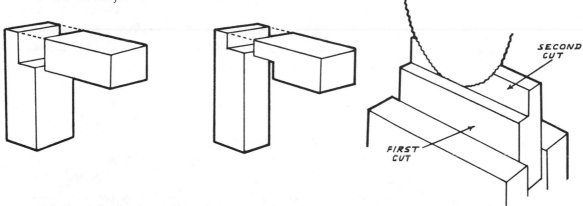

guideline along the edge of the wood at a point equal to the depth of the rabbet, set your saw blade to that depth and cut along the line.

The same procedure can be followed using a hand saw. In fact, it is a much safer procedure to saw out a rabbet than to risk breaking pieces of the board end with a chisel.

LAP JOINT   A lap joint is really a rabbet and a dado, or two large rabbets. It is used to save space as well as to provide strength. The aim of the lap joint, which is often found in chair rails and other parts of furniture, is to bring two pieces of wood together so that they overlap and make a strong joint that is no thicker than the wood itself. Thus, a lap joint is cut to a depth of one-half the thickness of both pieces of

Lap joints can be applied in numerous ways.

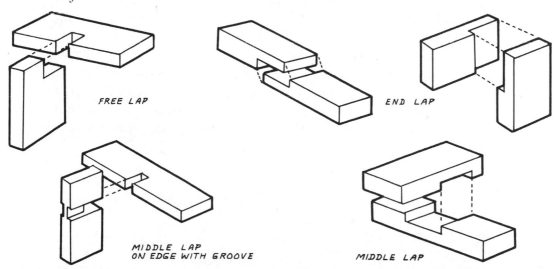

wood. It is usually used to join the ends of two narrow pieces to form a corner, but it can also be used to join boards together at their sides.

The dado blade is the quickest and most accurate tool for making a lap joint. You can also saw to the depth of half the wood thickness and then chisel out the waste material.

Preassembling Joints

When all the joints in your project have been cut, check each of them for smoothness. If you have been using a dado blade, usually nothing more needs to be done to them. But if you have done any chiseling, the inner surfaces of the joints will probably require sanding.

Next, assemble each joint and examine it minutely. You should not see any light coming through the joint. If you find daylight, either recut the joint or smooth it until all the matching surfaces touch properly. When all the joints meet with your satisfaction, you can begin assembling the project.

Gluing, Nailing and Screwing

The dadoes in any project offer both stability and strength, so whenever possible, assemble them first. If you are putting together a bookcase, and the shelves are dadoed while the top and bottom have rabbets, begin by putting the shelves together. Squirt a trail of glue in the dado and smear it along all three of the gluing surfaces, then insert the shelf end. Next, assemble the opposite end of the shelf in its dado. Then assemble all the other shelves and attach the rabbeted pieces. The rabbeted pieces must be nailed or clamped until the glue has hardened. You can, if you wish, secure any or all of the shelves with nails or screws as well as glue. Immediately wipe off any excess glue that has seeped out of the joints, using a rag dipped in warm water. If glue does not show at the seams, you have not put enough in the joint; if you wipe away the excess at once, you will have less trouble cleaning the wood and preparing it for its finish. Almost no finish or stain will cover a glue stain, and you cannot sand glue off wood. You have to scrape it off with a chisel blade or knife; sanding only drives the glue deeper into the wood fibers.

SUBASSEMBLIES

Subassemblies are units that are a part of your project but not indigenous to it. They include drawers and their frames, and doors and their frames. In constructing a cabinet, which might include both a drawer and a door or two, you would put together the cabinet and its shelves and then turn your attention to the doors and drawer, treating them almost as if they were separate projects.

Drawers

If you possess a router and dovetail template, you can—and should—make the age-old, time-honored dovetail joint in every corner of every drawer. You'll need about 60 seconds per joint to do the job. But dado and rabbet joints can be used with just as much effect. You can even use a butt joint, except that because of the dynamics of drawers, it is the least desirable method of assembly.

A drawer is a box that is normally operated by gripping a handle attached to its front panel and pulling it forward, then pushing it back again. These movements put tremendous pressure on the joints that hold the front of the drawer in position. In addition, the contents of the drawer slide back and forth, slamming first against the back panel, then against the front panel. If the contents are silk scarves, a wooden drawer will remain intact for years. But if you are storing gold ingots in that drawer, the front and back panels will be banged apart in short order.

Because of the constant pressures exerted on drawers, their joinery must be carefully thought out. The experience of several centuries of cabinetmakers around the world has developed preferred methods of assembly that will keep drawers together for years.

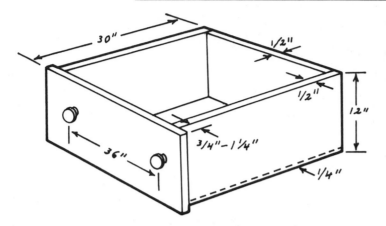

For the sake of convenience, the dimensions of a drawer should not exceed the dimensions shown here.

MATERIALS Drawers can be made of wood, plastic, metal, cardboard or practically any other material. With wood, ½" stock is traditionally used for the sides and back, ¼" stock for the bottom and ¾" stock for the front. These dimensions can be varied, of course— they would change if you were making a very small unit for holding jewelry, or a large tool drawer. The drawers in fine furniture tend to be made with hardwoods—principally oak—but pine, fir and plywood will work for storage.

JOINTS The back of any drawer must be joined so that it can resist the pressure of its contents slamming against it. Consequently, the back of the drawer should always be positioned between the sides and held there in either dadoes or a rabbet-dado combination. In other words, the back is rabbeted at both ends, and the rabbets are inserted in dadoes cut out of the sides, giving you four gluing surfaces. If necessary, use a butt joint that is glued and nailed or screwed through the outside of the sides. No matter what assembly you use, glue the back and, if possible, use some kind of metal fastener as well.

The bottom of a drawer must constantly support the full weight of whatever is inside the unit. Parenthetically, it also guarantees the squareness of the drawer, which is particularly important since the unit must fit snugly inside some form of cavity. The ideal system for holding a drawer bottom in place is to fit it into dadoes routed out of the bottom edges of all four sides. You can get away with routing just

*The three best joints to use when as-
sembling the sides and back of a
drawer.*

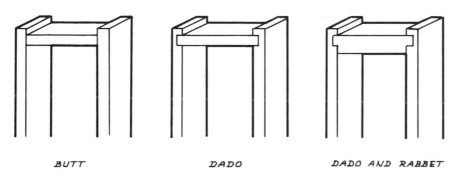

BUTT   DADO   DADO AND RABBET

the sides but ensure that the bottom will not fall out by extending it
over the bottom edge of the back and nailing it into the back. You can
also rabbet the bottom edges of the back and sides, and fit the bottom
into those; or you can attach the bottom flush to the bottom edges of
the sides and back. With the flush method you run the risk of losing
the bottom, so glue, then nail or screw it. But understand that the
weight of the drawer load will be pushing down in the direction of the
fasteners and will eventually shove them out of their holes.

*Joints used in assembling a drawer
bottom.*

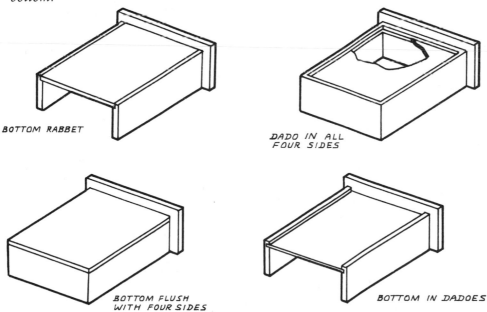

BOTTOM RABBET

DADO IN ALL
FOUR SIDES

BOTTOM FLUSH
WITH FOUR SIDES

BOTTOM IN DADOES

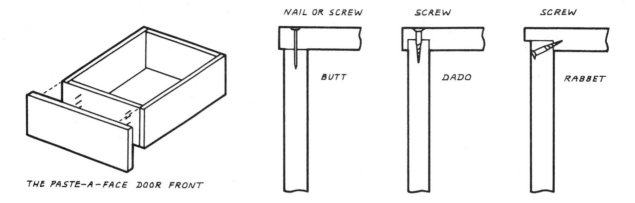

Four ways of attaching a drawer front to the sides and bottom.

THE PASTE-A-FACE DOOR FRONT

If the bottom is inserted in a four-sided dado, do not glue or nail it. Wood expands and contracts with every change in the weather, and if it is locked inside a four-way dado it will eventually split. Hardboard does not change much, so it can be glued.

Drawer fronts present some special problems because they are yanked and pushed, which tends to loosen their joints. The load inside slams against them, then backs away only to come rushing up against them again. Considering that end grains have no holding power, you can imagine how long a drawer front would last if you just nailed it to the front ends of the sides. If you must fasten it to the front ends of the sides, use screws and an extremely tough glue. You can improve the chances of keeping the front in place if you glue the drawer sides in dadoes routed into the back side of the front panel. By far the best system is to rabbet the sides of the drawer front, glue the drawer sides, then drive nails, or preferably screws, through the sides and into the front. You are still going into the end grains of the front piece, but at least the load will be against the shear line of the fasteners.

An alternative to the rabbet is to make the front out of two pieces of wood. The first piece is butt-joined between the sides where it is glued, then nailed or screwed. The second piece is then glued to the front of the first piece and also held in place with at least four screws driven through the first piece.

Note that the front of any drawer is almost always larger than the rest of the unit. If the unit is an overlapping drawer, the front is large enough to overlap the edges of the frame around the drawer. If a flush drawer, the front is still large enough to cover the guides and each side is no more than 1/16″ smaller than the cavity made by the frame.

DRAWER GUIDES   There are four ways of controlling a drawer as it slides in and out of its cavity. You can have guides on the sides or at the bottom corners; there can be one under the center of the bottom; or you can use metal tracks.

Side guides are square pieces of wood attached to the sides of the drawer frame which fit into oversized dadoes routed out of the sides of the drawer. Or there may be wooden rails glue-screwed to the sides of the drawer which serve the same function as dadoes. You can reverse this arrangement by having the guides attached to the drawer and the rails to the drawer frame.

Corner guides are strips of L-shaped wood attached to the lower corners of the frame so that the bottom edges of the drawer sides can slide along them.

A center guide is a grooved strip of wood glue-nailed to the bottom centerline of the drawer. The groove is a shade larger than a wooden rail nailed to the frame.

Drawers can have their guides positioned at the sides, bottom edges or center of the bottom.

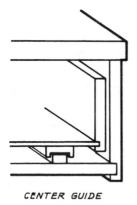

CENTER GUIDE

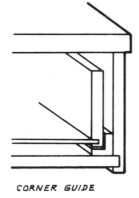

CORNER GUIDE

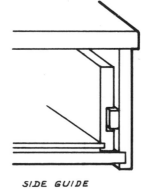

SIDE GUIDE

Finally, there is a variety of drawer-guide hardware available in most hardware stores. These consist of two metal tracks which are screwed to the sides of the drawer, and two metal guides which are screwed to the corresponding sides of the drawer frame. The tracks and guides consume $1/2''$ of space on each side, so the drawer must be made 1" narrower than its frame, and the front panel must extend at least $1/2''$ beyond each side to hide the tracks.

Metal tracks are great once you get them installed and working properly. But to do that, you must have an absolutely square drawer and a perfectly aligned frame with precisely $1/2''$ difference on both sides. If you have less than $1/2''$, the tracks will jam; if you have more than $1/2''$, the tracks will fall out of their guides.

DRAWER FRAMES   You can be a little sloppy about assembling just about any project except drawers and their frames; if you get either out of line, the drawer will most likely not work properly. The frames that hold a drawer can take several forms. You can build a simple box between $1/16''$ and $1/8''$ larger than the drawer. But that can consume a lot of wood and add considerable expense to your project. A more precarious but less expensive method is to build a frame using $1'' \times 2''$ stock. Be sure that the wood you use is as straight as possible. The frame consists of a series of vertical and horizontal rectangles or squares, and you must be very careful to get all the members of the frame positioned at exactly 90°. When that is finished, attach drawer guides with an equal amount of care.

Try to make your drawers first, then build the frames around them. It is infinitely easier to adjust several pieces of $1'' \times 2''$ wood strips than to adjust the unyielding boards of a drawer. This is particularly true if you are using metal drawer guides, which can present a time-consuming chore. The simplest method of assembly is to attach the guides to the sides of the drawer, then hold the drawer in place against one side of the incomplete frame and pin one rail in place. Insert the drawer in the one rail, then bring the opposite side of the frame against the free side and mark the position for the other rail. Pin the second rail in place with two screws and try out the drawer. The hardware has elongated screw holes so that you can move both the

Drawer frames must be carefully constructed so that they are as square in all directions as the drawers they hold.

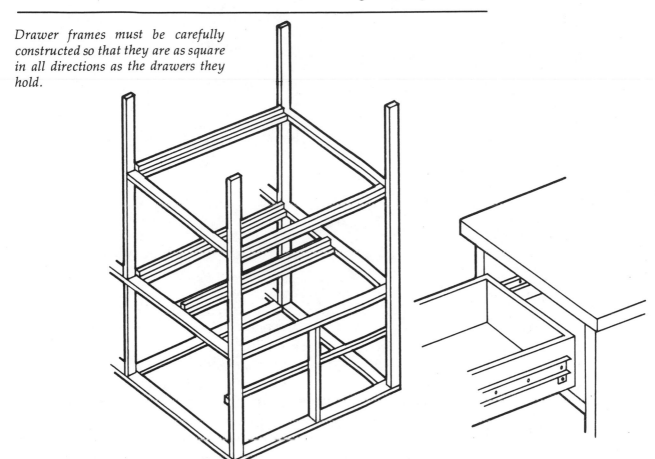

rails and the guides up and down or back and forth. You probably will have to spend some time fooling around with them before the drawer works perfectly. When it does work, permanently attach the free side of the frame.

Doors and Door Frames

Doors can be sliding, folding, hinged, solid or frame-and-panel. They can also be lipped, flush or overlapping. As with drawers, it is easier to construct the door and then fit the frame around it than the other way around.

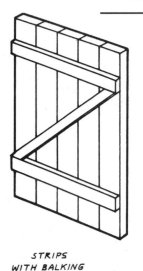

STRIPS
WITH BALKING

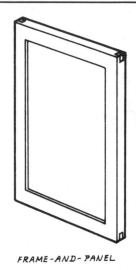

FRAME-AND-PANEL

Braces can be attached to the back or both the front and back of a solid door to keep it from warping. Frame-and-panel doors tend to warp much less than solid wood panels.

DOOR CONSTRUCTION If the unit is small enough, you can cut a piece of plywood or even particleboard to the size you wish and hang it on hinges over the front of a cabinet, and it will serve you for years without warping noticeably. Most of the cabinet doors in your kitchen are made from plywood. But if you use a single, wide piece of softwood or hardwood, sooner or later it will warp and stop closing properly. You may be able to retard the inevitable warping by adding a crosspiece or two on the top and bottom of the inside of the door.

You can also assemble a door by gluing together several strips of narrow wood and backing them with crosspieces. Because they are narrow, the strips will warp less noticeably and the door will work longer before it must be replaced or repaired.

The time-honored method of making an almost warp-proof door is to construct a frame made of wood that is ¾" to 2½" thick, and then dado a ⅛"- to ½"-thick panel inside the frame. The frame must be constructed with some intricate joinery like mortise and tenons, dowels, rabbets, and dadoes. Also, the edges must be beveled slightly and the whole frame has to be absolutely square. To do all this properly, you should have at your command at least a radial arm or table saw, a joiner-planer and/or stationary sanding machine, a drill stand (or,

Doors can be hung flush inside their
frames (A), be lipped over the frame
(B), or fully overlap the frame (C).

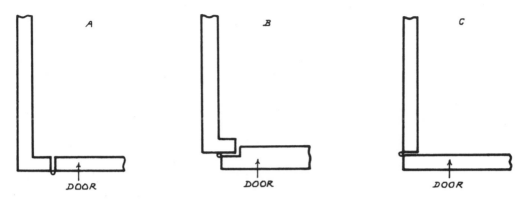

even better, a drill press), a mortise chisel, doweling jig or dowel centering pins, bar clamps and a considerable amount of time. Not many storage areas are worth the effort.

HANGING DOORS   The majority of cabinets needed around the average home are small enough to use solid plywood doors, which are usually hinged to the face of the cabinet in one of three ways. They can fit flush inside their frames just as all the room doors in your house do. They can be lipped, which requires that you cut a rabbet out of the inside edges of the door so that part of the door fits inside the frame and the edge closes against the face of the frame. Or they can be fully overlapping, in which case they are hinged against the face of the frame.

You can choose from an almost infinite number of hinges. There are face hinges which come with curves and angles that will fit around your rabbets and offer all manner of decorative designs in the process. You can use pivot hinges which hold the door at its top and bottom edges. And, of course, you can use a standard leaf hinge that is screwed into the edges of the frame and door.

Hinges can be tough to attach, particularly the traditional barrel hinges used to hang closet doors. The door edge and also the frame should be dadoed just deeply enough so that the hinge leaf lies flush with the wood. If the dadoes are too deep or the mortise is crooked, the door will not close properly. The best procedure is to mortise the door and attach the hinges with a single screw in each leaf. Then stand the door in its frame and mark the position of each hinge on the frame. Mortise the frame and hang the door using one screw in each hinge. Try the door. If it works properly, put in the rest of the screws and count your blessings. If it does not work, you will have to put shims under the hinges, deepen the hinge mortises, shave the edges of the door or reposition the whole thing.

If you are hanging a closet door and must also build the frame for it, buy a hollow-core door of the size you want, and set up the rough frame members plus the top and hinge-side door jambs. Hang the door, then put the lock-side jamb in place. You may have to shim the jamb, but that is quicker and easier than fooling around with the hinges.

SLIDING DOORS   Sliding doors can be used on cabinets or for closets. In either case, you can buy wooden or metal tracks which are screwed into place at the top and bottom of the door frame. The doors are cut ⅜″ shorter than the distance from the bottom of the top track to

Sliding cabinet doors are positioned in dadoes. When the sliding door reaches closet proportions, it must be suspended from wheels that roll inside a track across the top of the door frame.

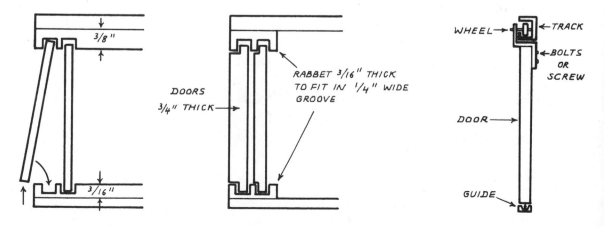

the bottom of the bottom track. The track grooves are normally ¼″ wide, so if the doors are thicker than that they will have to be rabbeted down until they can slide in the grooves. You can, of course, skip the tracks and simply rout out the top and bottom members of the front edges of a cabinet and place the sliding doors in the grooves. The top grooves should be slightly deeper than the bottom ones so that when you insert the doors you can push them upward enough to swing them over the lip of the bottom and drop them down into the bottom grooves.

BIFOLD DOORS   Bifolds are a nice space saver and in tight areas you may have to use them, but they are a trauma to install. First, you have to buy a set of bifold hardware which includes pivot hinges, wheels, guides, door pulls and tracks. The set comes with detailed, hard-to-follow instructions.

But the instructions are only a minor annoyance compared to the real problem—bifold doors must be fitted in an absolutely square enclosure. That means the tracks must be parallel to each other and also form a right angle with the door jambs. To begin with, no two walls in any house ever come together at a precise right angle. One side of a door opening can be several degrees off vertical in three directions at once, and the other side can easily be several degrees off in three other directions. If you get all six of those directions straightened out by building new door jambs, you will probably discover that the floor and ceiling of your house are nowhere near parallel to each other. You can set a level top jamb with no problem—but then step back and look at it. It may be parallel with the earth, but if it is off-line visually, everybody is going to say, "Why did you hang that bifold so crookedly?" Think long and hard before you decide to hang bifold doors.

When you have cut the wood, made the joints and assembled all of the drawers and doors, you have finished the construction of your project. Now the long part of your task begins. Putting a proper finish on most projects usually requires more time than all the work you have done so far.

SIX

Finishing

STORAGE SPACE IS BY AND LARGE MEANT TO BE unnoticed. It fills out-of-the-way corners, groans under loads of goods behind locked doors, is even sometimes artfully concealed in distant rooms of the house. But very often some part of the storage is left standing naked before the passing world. It may be only a door or a handle, or it might be an entire cabinet. Whatever part is visible you will want to make as compatible with its surroundings as possible. Consequently, plywood end grains must be covered; rough planking should be highlighted or covered under a layer or two of paint; a door on the face of a kitchen cabinet should look like all the other doors in the room.

There are two practical reasons for going to the effort to finish your storage projects. Dirt accumulating on bare, unfinished wood grinds its way into the fibers and the wood eventually becomes extremely difficult to clean. If you attack naked wood with a sponge and soapy water, what you will get is damp dirty wood; somehow the more you scrub, the deeper the dirt and grime go. Cleaning wood, especially shelves, is considerably easier if there is a coat of varnish or paint sealing the wood's naturally open pores.

The other practical reason for finishing wood: a finish, any finish, protects it from the elements. A coat or two of paint helps fight off humidity and moisture, and reduces the amount of swelling and shrinking that occur every time wood responds to changes in the weather.

After constructing a project with shelves, it is dangerous to immediately start loading them with everything you have designed them to hold. You unclutter your surroundings by filling those shelves, which then disappear—out of sight, out of mind. Try to resist the temptation to forget about the shelves at least long enough to get a coat of something on the wood first.

An ideal finish is the one on your dining room table or the legs of your living room couch. It was achieved by someone who spent hours and hours sanding, filling defects in the wood, sanding, applying a wood sealer, sanding, applying a primer coat, sanding, putting on a first coat, sanding, applying a second coat, sanding, applying a third coat, sanding, applying a final coat and rubbing the finish to its ultimate polish with pumice and then rottenstone. It takes time, lots of it, and unless you are doing a hardwood chiffonier for your formal dining room, it is not all necessary.

THE NATURE OF SOFTWOODS

Pine and fir (and plywood, which is made with both) are porous. Their fibers are soft and very open, and it takes special thick liquids to soak into the wood and fill the spaces between the fibers. You can do this with several layers of paint, or you can use a sealer-filler, which is also a kind of paint, and save yourself considerable work.

Any liquid that you put on a softwood tends to raise the fibers, and it takes several coats before the finish dries with anything approaching smoothness. So each coat must be lightly sanded, enough to make it feel smooth. The final coat, which will probably be rough to the touch, should also be sanded. But since you don't want to ruin the sheen, use pumice or rottenstone, both of which will smooth the last coat.

One point about fir to bear in mind from the beginning: it has a grain that looks and feels like a series of swirling ridges. The ridges rise above the surface of the wood, and they will always rise above it. You can sand them smooth, but as soon as anything wet is applied to them they pop right up again. Fir is a little less expensive than pine and equally strong, so you can save money by using it for shelving or wherever the ridges will not be important to the looks of the project.

But if you try to make a cabinet door out of fir plywood, you will be a long time hiding the grain, and there is no telling how much all that extra paint will cost you.

BASIC FINISHING MATERIALS

As far as storage is concerned, the finish materials you are most likely to need are stains, sealers or fillers, shellac, varnish and paint. Incidentally, sealers, fillers, primers and sealer-fillers are all pretty much the same material.

Stains

Stains do not cover the surface of any wood. They are made to penetrate it, to soak through the fibers, where they accent the grain as well as color it. You can buy stains in almost any color, and they can be mixed with each other to make still more colors. You can also take a tube of artist's oil and squirt that into a stain to change its hue. Be careful though—the color you see in the can is never exactly what you will get after it soaks into a piece of wood.

You can also buy wood stains advertised as one-coat finishers. They have wax, varnish and/or wood sealer mixed in with them, but they are so busy trying to be two or three things at once that they don't stain, varnish or seal anything particularly well. The commercial stains also tend to be a little thin and almost always produce a color drastically lighter than the one shown on the can's label. You have some options when this happens. You can keep applying coats of stain and the color will gradually darken. You can also mix in artist's oils. Or you can make your own stain. Buy a can of clear, penetrating oil stain, a tube of burnt sienna and a tube of burnt umber. Together they will create any brown tint you wish. Mix the colors into the oil until you have the color you want, but test it on a scrap piece of wood before putting it on your project.

Apply a stain by dipping a clean, soft cloth into it and rubbing it into the surface of the wood. Let it stand for an hour or two, then rub off any excess oil you find on the surface of the wood. If you do not wipe the wood, it will continue to get darker and darker. In fact, you can literally watch it change color; when it attains the shade you want, wipe it. If the color gets too dark, you can lighten it by wiping the surface of the wood with pure turpentine. Allow the stain to dry for at least 24 hours before putting any other finishing material on top of it.

Sealers

The substance to put on top of a stain first is a clear wood sealer (filler). Wood is hardly a perfect material. It has both hard and soft spots all over it, which you can readily discern as soon as you put any finish on it. You will notice that a coat of varnish, for example, dries very quickly in some places and remains tacky for longer periods of time in others. The dry spots occur where the fibers are more open and able to soak up more of the varnish than the spots that are more compressed.

The objective of using a clear wood sealer is to fill in the hard and soft spots and even out the texture of the wood. Like stain, a sealer-filler soaks into the fibers of the wood; if it does its task properly, you will find it gives the surface a satiny feel.

Apply the sealer with a brush or rag, and give it 24 hours to dry thoroughly. At that point, sand the wood with a fine-grit abrasive. With a good sealer, it takes nothing more than a few swipes of the abrasive to do all the sanding needed. The sealer, by the way, will eliminate at least one of the finish coats you would ordinarily need to properly finish a piece of fir or pine.

Shellac

One of the materials you can use as a primer-sealer on plywood is shellac. It works extremely well under paint or varnish, but it comes in only two colors (orange and white), both of which darken any wood.

Shellac is made of the resinous secretions of the Asian lac insect mixed with denatured alcohol. How much lac is used is indicated on the can label as the "cut" of the shellac. A two-pound cut means that two pounds of lac was mixed with one gallon of alcohol; a three-pound cut is three pounds of lac with a gallon of alcohol, and so on. Every can of shellac comes with a mixing chart on its label which tells you how much alcohol to add in order to change the cut ratio. You want a three-pound cut when applying shellac to plywood, so you may have to add some alcohol to the can you have purchased.

Never shake shellac; only stir it. Shaking causes bubbles which remain on the wood and harden into an uneven finish. You can apply shellac with a bristle brush or a foam rubber pad, but in either case, brush the shellac into the wood with long, even strokes. You can brush in any direction because shellac fills in the brush marks as it dries. A three-pound cut will be dry in about two hours, and then can be rubbed down with fine steel wool or extra-fine sandpaper; after this a second coat is applied. Two coats of shellac will provide an excellent base for a varnish top coat. Alternatively, you can keep on applying shellac until you have a glossy finish. If the final coat is too glossy, you can dull it by lightly rubbing with fine steel wool.

Varnish

Varnish is made up of resins, linseed oil, drying agents and enough turpentine to make it flow smoothly. It is available in flat finish as well as satin, medium and high glosses, and is clear. Varnishes have always been easy to apply and slow to dry. While they provide a hard finish, heat will often blister them and many liquids will leave a stain on them. But now we have polyurethane.

The urethanes are all varnishes. They can be applied as easily as regular varnish, but they dry faster, resist water, alcohol and dirt, and are so tough their primary use is as a finish on floors. Their only drawback is that they will not go over shellac or most sealers. You have to use a special polyurethane primer, or thin the first coat of urethane with turpentine and use that as your sealer.

Most raw softwoods need at least two coats of varnish applied over a sealer. Do not shake varnish; it will bubble. You can apply varnish with a rag, a roller, a bristle brush or, best of all, with a foam rubber pad. The pads leave no brush strokes, hold a maximum of varnish which can be flowed onto the work, and they are disposable.

When you are using a brush, dip it into the varnish and tap the end of the brush against the rim of the can. Do not rub the brush over the rim; this causes bubbles. Apply the varnish in long, flowing strokes with the grain of the wood, overlapping each stroke slightly. If you are wiping on the varnish, fold a clean, lint-free cloth into a pad and dip it in the can, then spread the varnish on with the same long, flowing strokes.

Varnish must be sanded between coats. Use a superfine-grit abrasive, and abrade the surface only enough to remove all of the sheen from the varnish. Then wipe the surface with a tack rag and apply the next coat.

TACK RAGS   Varnish in particular, but every type of finish material will have no chance of drying to a smooth finish if it is applied over a rough surface. You can wipe a piece of wood with clean rags and even a damp rag, and still not pick up anywhere near all of the dust on the wood. You must also wipe it with a tack rag.

You can buy tack rags at any paint-supply store, but you can also make one by sprinkling a clean, lint-free cloth with a solution of varnish diluted by 25% turpentine. You can get along without the varnish, but turpentine by itself is not quite as effective. Fold the cloth and wring it almost dry, then wipe the entire surface with it. You should use a tack rag to clean any surface, but particularly after you have sanded a coat of paint or varnish.

Enamel and Other Paints

Enamel is varnish with a pigment added. Everything you would do or not do with varnish applies to enamel. When you decide to paint the outside of a cabinet or the door of a closet, select an oil-based enamel. Sand the surfaces to be painted, wipe them with a tack rag and put on a coat of sealer. Sand the sealer, wipe it with a tack rag, and apply the first coat of enamel; when it is dry, sand it until the sheen is gone. Then wipe it with a tack rag and apply the second finish coat. In most cases that should be enough. If it is not, put on another coat or two until you are satisfied.

The interiors of storage, such as inner walls and shelves, can be covered with flat water-based paints or with enamel. The enamel will withstand more cleaning, but then how many times will you wash the inside walls of your sports cabinet? Shelves will collect dust, but they are not washed very often either; the purpose of painting them is really to help them stay clean and to preserve the wood.

The water-based paints are easiest to use because they are water soluble, and so make it easier to clean yourself and your equipment. They can be applied with brushes, rollers and paint pads. Pads are so fast and efficient, they should be your first choice.

THE FINAL STEP: HAND-RUBBING

Seven days after you have applied the last coat of enamel or varnish to a project, the finish will have hardened sufficiently to be given its final rubbing. Mix a paste of water or motor oil and rottenstone, which is a gray powder you can purchase at any paint store. Dip a heavy, folded cloth into the mixture and "sand" the surface with long, even strokes, going with the grain of the wood and using moderate pressure. Stroke the finish eight or nine times, and then use a clean cloth to wipe off excess paste. Keep wiping and rubbing, using successive clean rags, until the finish squeaks. If you used motor oil, the finish will be glossy. With water, the finish will be a dull matte.

SEVEN

Tips, Hints and Flourishes

CERTAIN STORAGE MAY REQUIRE SPECIAL WORKING techniques or unique decorative effects. There can arise unusual problems in hanging shelves or building the base of a freestanding cabinet to fit around the room baseboard and stand flush against a wall. There may be a space problem that could be conveniently solved with an unusual design of hardware. Here are some ways of dealing with special problems; variations of these themes might apply to the situation confronting you.

BENDING WOOD

The heavy hitters in the furniture industry bend both hardwoods and softwoods with huge steam ovens and hydraulically controlled wood presses. The wood is steamed until it is pliable, cranked and clamped into whatever shape is desired and then allowed to dry. If you are building some storage that requires you to bend a piece of wood and you don't happen to own a furniture factory, you will have to resort to one or two more rudimentary methods, kerfing or laminating.

Kerfing

A kerf is the slot left in a piece of wood by a saw blade. In principle, if you cut a series of evenly spaced kerfs in any piece of

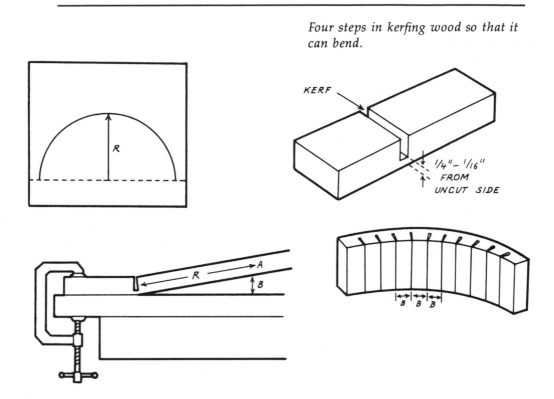

Four steps in kerfing wood so that it can bend.

wood, you can then bend that wood into almost any radius. But you cannot put kerfs into wood randomly. The procedure below works particularly well with plywood, where your kerfs can be exactly deep enough to cut through all but the face veneer.

1. Determine the radius of the curve you want to bend your wood around.

2. Near the middle of the unseen side of the stock you are bending, cut one kerf across the wood to a depth of $1/4''$ to $1/16''$ from the face of the board.

3. Clamp one end of the board to a tabletop. Bend the free end upward until the edges of the saw cut touch, and prop the wood in place with a block of wood.

4. Along the raised side of the board, mark off the length of the radius (R) from the edge of the kerf. At the end point of the

radius (A) measure the distance of the face side of the board to the tabletop (B). That measurement (B) becomes the distance between each kerf.

5. Unclamp the board and cut a series of equally deep kerfs the full length of the bend.

6. Fill each kerf with a strong glue such as one of the acrylics or resorcinols.

7. Slowly bend the board around the curve and attach it with clamps or fasteners. If the piece is small enough and the radius is very tight, you can soften the wood by holding it over a steaming teakettle, but in most cases this is not necessary.

Admittedly, you are weakening the wood considerably by kerfing it, but if the glue you use in each slot is a good one, your piece should be as strong as ever.

Laminating

The strongest method of bending wood is laminating several thin strips of stock together. This is based on the old bundle-of-faggots-are-hard-to-break theory, and it works. Each strip of wood must be thin enough to bend around the curve you have in mind. In most instances, that would be between ⅛" and ¹/₁₆" thick. Lauan plywood, which is sold in 4'×8' or 3'×7' sheets, comes in these thicknesses.

Apply a smooth layer of strong glue over every part of each strip, then bend the strips one at a time around the curve and clamp them together until the glue dries. You can create the sides of a curved tray, make the edges of a counter top, even use ¼"-thick plywood strips to manufacture circular-stair banisters.

If the bend is too tight for the thickness of the wood, steam it and then clamp it in place to dry. But do not try gluing damp wood to itself—the glue won't hold.

Laminating several thin strips of wood will produce a rigid structure.

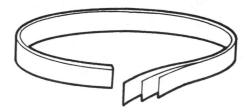

PLASTIC LAMINATES

Kitchen counter tops, bathroom sink vanities, children's furniture and any number of other projects can be built of inexpensive plywood or, better still, of particleboard (which is even cheaper) and then covered with any of the plastic laminates sold at lumberyards and home-improvement centers.

The laminates are constructed of layers of heavy kraft paper impregnated with plastic resins and then bonded under intense heat and pressure until a hard, brittle surface develops. Since the material is completely man-made, the manufacturer has total control of his product and therefore can offer an incredible array of patterns and sizes. Panel dimensions range from 2' to 5' wide and 6' to 12' long, with thicknesses of $1/16"$, $1/20"$ and $1/32"$. There are three basic grades to consider when using plastic laminates for storage projects.

Standard grade laminate is $1/16"$ thick, can be used for any vertical surface and can be bent to a 9" radius. If you heat the material to 360°F, you can curve it as tightly as a $2\frac{1}{2}"$ radius.

Postforming grades are $1/20"$ thick and can be heated to go around almost any curve, which makes them excellent for edging almost anything.

Vertical grades are $1/32"$ thick and are supposed to be used only on vertical surfaces such as doors, walls or cabinet sides. If you cut this type into narrow strips or buy it that way, it is called edge banding and is used to cover counter-top edges.

All of the laminates must be fully supported. They are thin and brittle and are designed to be both decorative and extremely durable. But they have to be pasted to a core of solid wood, plywood, particleboard or even hardboard if they are to be used on a horizontal surface such as a counter top; plywood should be at least $3/4"$ thick and particleboard at least $5/8"$. If you are using laminates vertically, say to line a closet, you should use plywood or particleboard at least $1/2"$ thick or $3/16"$ hardboard as your backing.

Fir, by the way, is not a good backing material. The high ridges in fir grain will either show through the laminate or cause pockets in the low spots where the laminate does not adhere.

You can use practically any glue to hold plastic laminate to its core, but all of the glues except contact cement require that the project be clamped until it dries. So use contact cement, as most professionals do. Whatever glue you select, follow the instructions carefully.

Cutting Laminates

Never cut any laminate unless it is fully supported. Since the laminates come in large pieces, you will have to reduce the panels with two or three rough cuts first. In making those cuts you may cause considerable chipping along the cut line, so leave yourself at least ½" of scrap material so that you will have ample material for trimming. You can mark your guidelines on the shiny side of the laminate with a grease pencil, which can easily be rubbed off later.

If you are using a power saw or a router to cut laminate, put on your carbide blade or bit. The resins in laminate are tough on standard steel blades, and aside from making your sawing a chore, you will chip every inch of material you cut. With any of the stationary power tools or a router, cut with the good side *up*, and take particular care that the material is fully and firmly supported.

A portable circular saw will cut laminate admirably, but the good side should be *down* and the material well supported. It is not a bad idea to place a piece of scrap wood underneath the face side of the laminate and saw through that as well.

You can hand-saw laminate using a metal hacksaw with at least 32 teeth per inch or a crosscut saw with 12 or more teeth per inch. In a pinch, score the face of the laminate with the point of an ice pick or awl, digging about halfway through the material, then bend the laminate upward to break off the waste material.

Laminates can also be drilled, but use sharp bits and go very slowly through the decorative side of the material first. Keep the work well supported. It is possible, but highly improbable, that sometime you will make a cut in a laminate without some chipping.

Gluing Laminates

In order to glue laminate to a project, you need plastic wood or wood putty, a can of contact cement, a glue spreader (a stick, piece of metal, brush, etc.) a piece of waxed or heavy brown paper, a hand roller (a rolling pin is fine), a portable router or a plane, and a flat-mill file. What you do with this strange conglomerate is:

1. Cut the laminate so that it is about ¼" larger in all directions than the core it is covering.

2. Fill the core to which you intend to glue the laminate with plastic wood or wood putty, and then sand the surface so that it is even. Any holes, gouges, splits or dents will become places the laminate does not adhere to.

3. Apply contact cement to both the back of the laminate and the surface of the core, and allow it to dry for 15 or 20 minutes. The cement is dry when you can slide a piece of waxed or brown paper over it without its sticking.

4. Place the waxed or brown paper on the core, leaving about 1" of the core uncovered, and align one edge of the laminate with an edge of the core.

5. Press the laminate down on the core. The glued surfaces will bond immediately; if the two pieces are not properly aligned, you are about to have a crooked piece of laminate on your project. So be precise.

6. Slide the paper out from between the laminate and its core, pressing the laminate down with your hands as you go. There is no hurry as long as the paper separates the glued surfaces. The cement will take hours before it dries too much to bond, unless it touches some other surface with cement on it.

Contact cement bonds instantly and solidly, so be very careful that the laminate is correctly aligned with the core you are gluing it to.

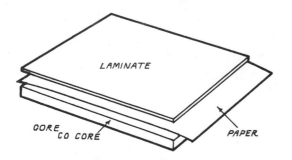

LAMINATE

CORE
CO CORE

PAPER

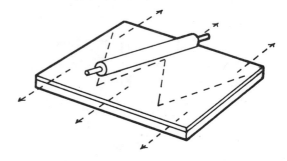

When gluing laminate to a project, begin with the pieces that will be seen last so that the maximum number of laminate edges will be covered.

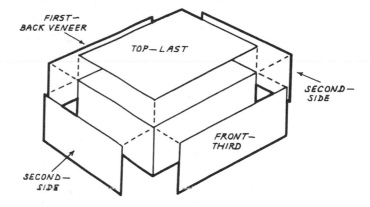

7. When the laminate is in place, roller it. Begin in the center and roller diagonally toward the edges. Then lean heavily on your roller and go along each of the edges. Alternatively, place a small block of wood on the laminate and tap it with your hammer. With either method, cover every square inch of the material.

8. You should have excess laminate hanging over all or most of the edges of the project. Plane it off or, better yet, use a portable router fitted with a straight bit and a laminate trimmer attachment. The attachment allows you to trim the edges and bevel the laminate simultaneously, and the router rotates at such a high speed that the laminate will not chip in the process.

The correct procedure for laminating, say, a cabinet, is to first apply laminate to the surfaces that will be seen the least. Thus you do the back first, then the sides, then the front, then the edges of the top, and finally the top. In each instance, trim all of the edges flush so that you can overlap them with the next piece.

Laminating Edges

Unless you are edge-banding, that is, putting laminate on the edges of the core, projects that are laminated always have their edges treated last. You can purchase either wood or metal edging or molding, and glue or glue-nail it to the edges.

If you are edge-banding and you must go around some curves, use a postforming grade of laminate, which is $^1/_{20}''$ thick and will, when heated to about 300°F, go around all sorts of curves. Cut the laminate into strips that are slightly wider than the edge you are covering and mark the face of the laminate with a crayon. Apply contact cement and, when it is dry, hold a heat lamp near the laminate; when the crayon melts, you can assume the laminate has reached the proper temperature. Put on asbestos gloves and push the laminate around the curve, then roller it.

When joining your edge-banding to the edge of, say, a counter top trim off the excess with a hacksaw or router, but be certain that the edge of the laminate is exactly level with the top of the core material. Make doubly sure that you use plenty of glue, and roller the edges until your arms get tired. It is the edges that come loose soonest, usually because they were underglued.

The bevel you notice around the top of professionally laminated counter tops is shaped from the top piece of laminate with a router and laminate trimmer attachment.

TIPS ON STABILIZING

It is quite possible to design and build a cabinet or bookcase that has dadoed shelves, is magnificently finished and looks great in every respect—but it wiggles. The surest way of stabilizing such a unit is to add a full back to it.

A piece of casework can be stabilized with almost any kind of back that touches two or more sides.

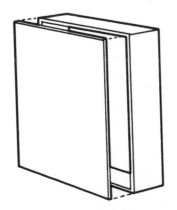 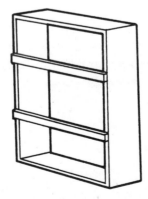 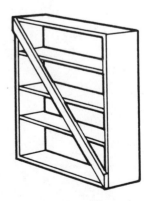

Backing

If the back is cut from a piece of hardboard or plywood and its four sides are truly at right angles to each other, it will keep the project both rigid and absolutely square. When you cut the back, try to use two of the edges and one existing 90° corner of the panel—but don't be sloppy about the other two edges.

There are several ways of attaching the back. The easiest is to put glue on the back edges of every member of the project, then align the back along the top of the piece and nail it in place at each corner. Next, align either adjacent edge with one of the project sides and tack that down. From there on, every outside member should be in line with the edges of the back, and you should put nails through the back into every part it touches.

However, when you lay a bookcase or cabinet face down and then completely cover its back with a piece of hardwood or plywood, you have no idea exactly where the shelves are. So before you cover the project, stand the back piece on edge and align it with a side of the project. Then mark the center of each shelf on the back piece. Now turn the back piece over and align it with the opposite side of the project. Mark the center of each shelf on that side. When you put the back on the project, be sure your pencil marks are showing (it's amazing how easy it is to mark a back and then glue it with the marked side against the project). When you begin nailing the back, place a straightedge between each of your pencil marks and place the point of each nail against it. All the nails should then enter the center of the cross members of the project.

Before glue-nailing a back in place, mark the position of all the members you intend to nail into.

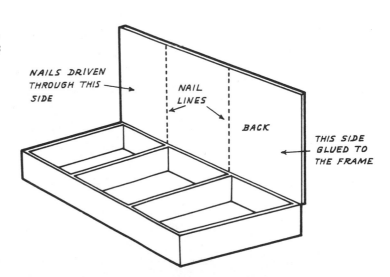

NAILS DRIVEN THROUGH THIS SIDE

NAIL LINES

BACK

THIS SIDE GLUED TO THE FRAME

A back does not have to fully cover a project to stabilize it. If you want a project only partially backed, try to catch at least two of the corners. A strip of hardboard between the top or bottom and one or two shelves, for example, will do wonders for stabilizing a bookcase. You can also attach a board or a piece of 1"×2" stock diagonally across the back from a top corner to the opposite bottom corner. If you go straight into the corner, at least the point of the strip will butt against the sides and/or horizontal members.

Backs, whether they are full or only partial, can be glue-nailed to the edges of the unit. They can also be hidden inside a rabbet that is about one-half the thickness of member edges. Of course, if your project is destined to be nailed into a corner or against a wall and you are not concerned with dust getting into the back of it, it is not necessary to add any back at all.

GETTING AROUND BASEBOARDS

There is some kind of baseboard in every room covering the joint between the floor and the walls. Baseboards can vary in height from ¾" to several feet. By and large they will be ¾" or 1" thick, although there may be a second piece of molding, called a shoe, nailed to the floor at the bottom of the baseboard. The purpose of the shoe is to cover the joint between the baseboard and the floor, and it is usually put there because the floor is uneven and the joint has opened up until it is practically a hole.

The problem with baseboards is that they can force a cabinet or shelf case to stand as much as 2" away from the wall because the case can get only as close to the wall as the baseboard (and sometimes its shoe) will allow it. You could remove the baseboard, but that would leave a pretty unsightly strip of unpainted or unfinished wall. Your alternative is to cut notches in the bottom back edges of your storage units. The notch need be only as deep as the thickness of the baseboard and only as long as the baseboard is high. If you have a saber saw, you can cut the notch so that it follows the curves of the baseboard molding.

Cutting a notch does not sound as though it would get you into much trouble, but it actually can cause a lot of extra work. To begin with, if you notch the bottom of a bookcase so it will fit around a 6"-high baseboard which is 1" thick, your bottom shelf will have to be ripped to a width 1" narrower than the other shelves in the case. Then, if you intend to have a back on the bookcase, it must end at the baseboard notch. You can put a strip across the back of the notch, but you will have a hole between the two backs. You can then fill the hole by cutting the lower back so that it extends up inside the case by ³/₄", then nail a strip of wood between the two backs.

Another way of getting around a baseboard is to inset the back and insert its sides in dadoes. The back would then be about 1" inside the cabinet, so you would have to reduce the width of all the shelves by that amount.

Some ways of getting around base-boards and molding.

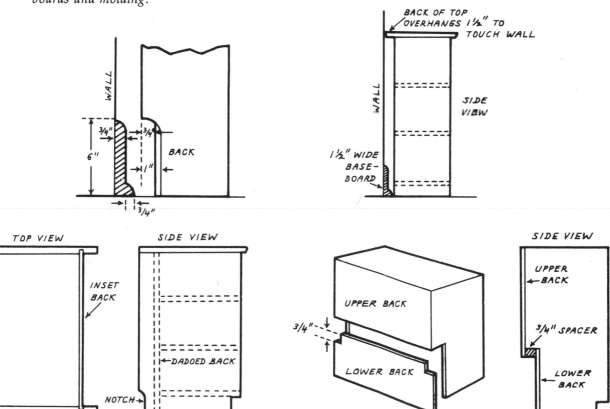

KICKPLATES

Kickplates are those inserts underneath the front of your kitchen and bathroom cabinets that let you belly up to the counters. They usually measure 3″ high and are recessed about 3¹/₂″, but you can adjust the dimensions. They are constructed by notching out the bottom front corners of the cabinet sides and nailing a vertical member between the sides that has its top edge level with the horizontal cut. The kickplate itself usually becomes a support for the bottom of the cabinet, which extends the 3″ or so in front of the kickplate to the leading edge of the unit. Kickplates are not necessary except in instances where anyone using the storage unit must be able to stand as close to it as possible. They have become a traditional and decorative feature, however, and most professionally made casework has them in one design or another.

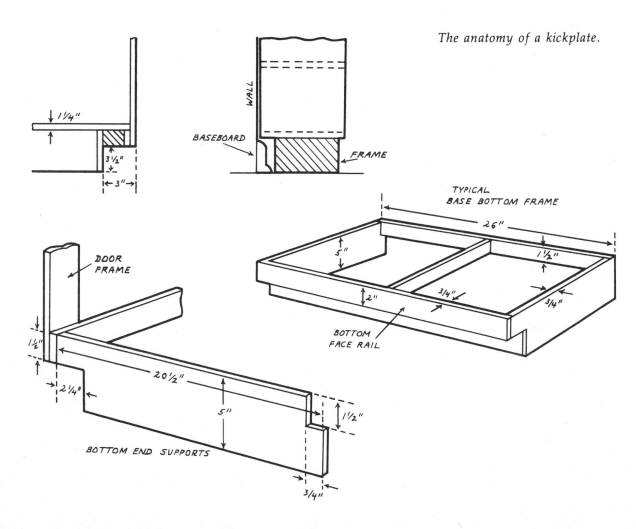

The anatomy of a kickplate.

HINTS FOR YOUR HANG-UPS

Shelves and cabinets are forever being hung from walls. Anytime you want to hang something of substantial weight, try to find a stud inside the wall to nail, screw or bolt into. In theory, you should find a piece of 2"×4" lumber standing every 16" inside any wall. There should be two of them nailed together around any door or window frame, and three of them anyplace two walls meet to form a corner. Don't count on it, though. Sometimes the studs are 24" or 36" apart, or they just aren't to be found.

So trying to locate a wall stud can be frustrating. You can tap the wall with your hammer and when the sound becomes a solid thud, hammer a small nail into the wall. If it catches on wood, you can measure 16" or 24" in either direction, drive another nail into the wall and hope to find another stud. If you punch a whole row of nails into a wall and get nothing but plaster, try examining the baseboard for nailheads. If you find any in the middle or upper half of the baseboard, go straight up and drill into the wall. There should be a stud there. When all these tricks fail, pull the baseboard off the wall, and all its inner secrets will be revealed to you—the base of every stud, the lath and where the contractor stopped plastering, 6" above the floor.

With a stud or two at hand, you can hang a full-backed cabinet by driving lag bolts or long screws into them. You can also hang large brackets to support the unit, or you can construct a remarkably simple system from 1"×2" stock. Cut two pieces of 1"×2" so that they fit tightly between the sides of the cabinet. Now rip both pieces down the center at a 45° angle. The top half of each piece is attached to the back of the cabinet, if there is one, with glue and screws or nails. Position the pieces so that you can anchor into the edge of the bottom and top horizontal members. If the cabinet has no back, the two pieces are fitted between the sides under the top and bottom horizontals. Screws or nails are driven into their ends through the cabinet sides, as well as down through the horizontal members. It is essential when attaching the top half of the 1"×2" stock that the wide side of the stock be facing outward so that the 45° miter angles upward toward the inside of the cabinet.

With the top half of the rails in place, hold the cabinet against the wall in exactly the position you want it to hang, and fit the bottom half of the rails against their corresponding top halves. Draw lines on the wall along the bottom edge of the rails (you will probably need all three of your hands, but it can be done). Remove the cabinet and rails from the wall, and place a level on the lines you have drawn. If the lines are off level, correct one of them and nail the bottom half of one of the rails to the wall studs with its wide side facing you. You should put a long nail through the rail and into every stud the rail crosses, but as long as you can hit at least two studs you are safe; the ends of the rail need not be nailed if they don't happen to correspond with a stud. If you're hanging a unit from a brick or masonry wall, attach the rail with anchors or plugs.

When one of the rails is installed, hold the cabinet against the wall and lower it until the top and bottom rails are fitted together. Hold the second bottom rail in place and draw a line along its bottom edge; then remove the cabinet and install the second rail. With securely anchored rails in the cabinet and against the wall, you can then hang the cabinet permanently or remove it anytime you wish merely by sliding it upward against the wall until the rails disengage.

The single disadvantage of hanging anything from rails is that if the unit has a back, the rails will hold it ¾″ away from the wall, and you may find that unsightly. You can hide the rails by extending the sides ¾″ past the cabinet back to cover the thickness of the 1″×2″ wood.

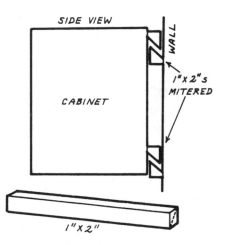

How to position the mitered halves of a 1″×2″ bracket.

Hanging Shelves

You can hang a shelf case using mitered 1"×2" rails or brackets or, if it has a back, with screws, nails or, better still, hanger bolts. You can also hang casework from the ceiling by attaching either pieces of wood or metal straps to the sides of the ceiling joists. Never hang something heavy by nailing into the bottom edge of a joist, because all of the weight will be pulling directly down on the nails and eventually pull them out of the wood. But if you can get the end of the hanger against the side of the joist and drive your fasteners through the side of the wood, the weight will be pulling across the shear of the nail or screw. You should also attach to the sides of the shelf or cabinet, not its top.

Some ways of hanging cabinets.

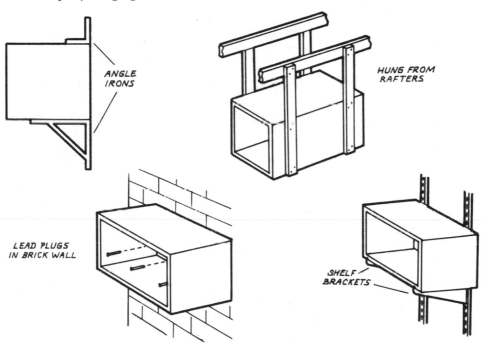

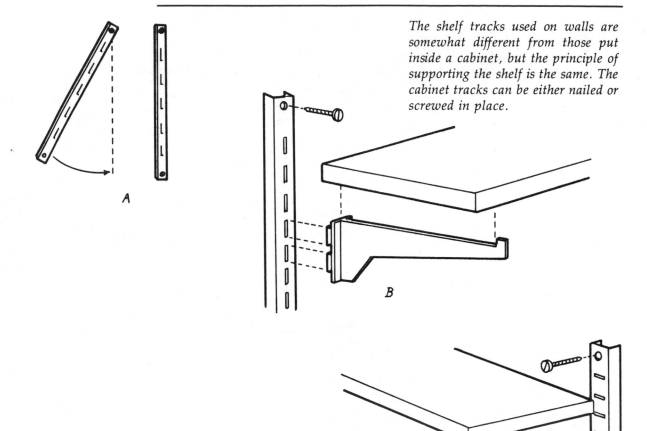

The shelf tracks used on walls are somewhat different from those put inside a cabinet, but the principle of supporting the shelf is the same. The cabinet tracks can be either nailed or screwed in place.

A

B

C

Shelves are often hung individually from tracks made of metal or plastic. The tracks and their brackets, which hold the shelves horizontally, are sold at both hardware and lumber outlets. The trick with tracks is to get them on the wall so they are parallel to each other and no more than 36" apart. If you are hanging them to studs they will be 32" apart, and that is better because pine board should not be asked to support much weight for more than 3' or it will begin to bow.

Hanging the tracks so they are parallel and plumb is not as hard as it sounds. Decide where the top of the track should be located, and put a screw through the topmost hole. Drive it into the wall until it is deep enough to hold the track, but do not tighten it; let the track swing freely until it comes to rest. The track is now hanging absolutely plumb with the earth's surface. The problem is it may look very crooked if the wall is not also plumb, which is most likely. If the track is so out of line with the rest of the room that it looks ridiculous, compromise by angling it just enough so that it *looks* straight. Then mark the other screw holes, swing the track out of your way and drill into the wall for screws or masonry anchors. All of the other tracks must then be measured from the top and bottom of the first track so that they are equidistant and parallel.

DECORATIVE EFFECTS

A cabinet or shelf case is nothing more than a box. In many instances the simple, clean lines of a box may be all you care about, in which case leave it that way. But be aware of what can happen visually to any box once you begin to decorate it. The principle behind the decoration is that the human eye, when presented with nothing but straight lines, begins seeking some sort of relief. That relief is provided once curves are introduced, and there are an almost infinite number of ways to add those curves.

Molding

You can build a box with shelves in it and then make it appear quite different simply by adding 1"×2" strips of wood around the edges. Or you can tack curved pieces of molding along the edges not only to cover them, but to create the relief of curves and thereby soften the harshness of straight lines and flat surfaces at right angles.

The business of adding pieces of wood to the edges of shelves has an economic advantage, too. You can use ½"-thick plywood for shelving, and it will support at least the same weight as a ¾" piece of pine or fir. But the plywood will bend considerably. On the other hand, ½" plywood is about two-thirds of the cost of ¾" softwood. You could make a shelf case from ½" plywood and then trim the leading edges of the shelves with 1"×2" pine strips, which will not only decorate the piece, but also keep the shelves from sagging under heavy weights.

One of the areas of a unit to treat with molding is the top. The top of a cabinet can have molding around its edges. You can also extend the top past the front and sides of the box by ½" or ¾" and tack your molding under the overhang. You can extend the top at just the front or sides, or you might extend it 1" or 1½" past the back to hold the unit as far away from the wall at the top as the baseboard holds it at the bottom.

A few of the ways a project can be decorated with molding and/or trim.

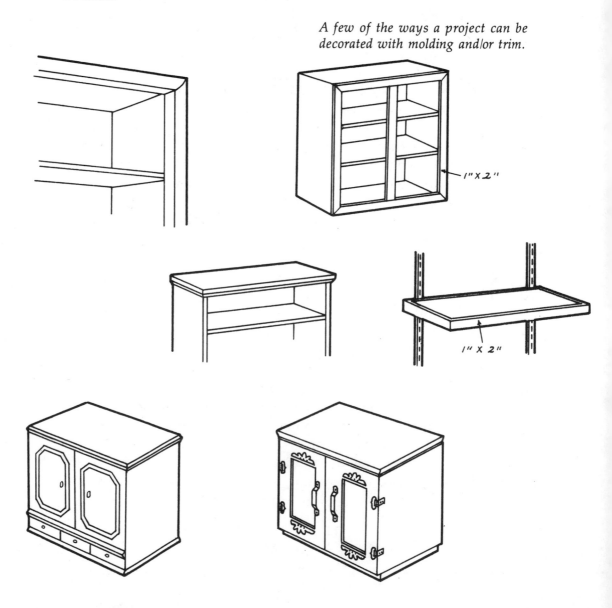

Another area that is often decorated is the face of a cabinet or closet door. Here you are confronted by a large, unrelieved flat surface. You can buy packages of precut trim that need only be glued or nailed to any surface to form a decorative frame. Or you can devise your own shapes and configurations from straight pieces of molding purchased at a local lumberyard.

Be careful, though. Don't put a lot of large, heavy molding all over a small, delicate cabinet. And don't underdo the decorative effect. Think about where your storage is located and the kind of decoration that will surround it. Consider the crown molding around the ceiling of the room. Look at the trim on the cabinets that are already in the room. Look at the furniture, and evaluate the molding and trim that is used on each piece. Then try to make your choice of molding compatible. The whole subject of trimming is pretty much a matter of taste, and no matter what your taste is, you will be able to find some sort of millwork to suit your needs. You can, without question, take any box and decorate it to look like anything from Roman or French Provincial to Greek, Scandinavian, Colonial or Neo-Salvation Army.

Hardware

Another common way of changing the look of things is with hardware. There are more kinds and designs of handles, pulls, hinges, latches, locks and catches than there are types of molding. You can get hinges that are decorative or hidden, simple handles and ornate ones, and even simple straps of metal (brass, copper, iron) that can be attached to the corners and edges of a cabinet to enhance the unit and help hold the joints together. Once again, personal taste and the surrounding objects should guide your choice. Obviously, you would not want to build some storage with a heavy Mediterranean look if it were surrounded by delicate French Provincial furniture or simple Danish modern.

A considerable amount of special hardware is now available that can be invaluable to your storage projects. You can purchase whole wire racks that are fitted on the inside of a closet door to become a removable shelf unit. There are sliding clothes racks; wire pot hooks that hang inside a cabinet and can be pulled out whenever you need a pot or pan; hardware for making lazy Susans; and a host of other oddball specialty items. Look for them in large home centers, department stores or specialty outlets. If you find one you think will fit into your storage plans, buy it. All of these units are useful, but not exactly best sellers, and they may not be available in six months, when you finally get around to tackling that storage project you have in mind.

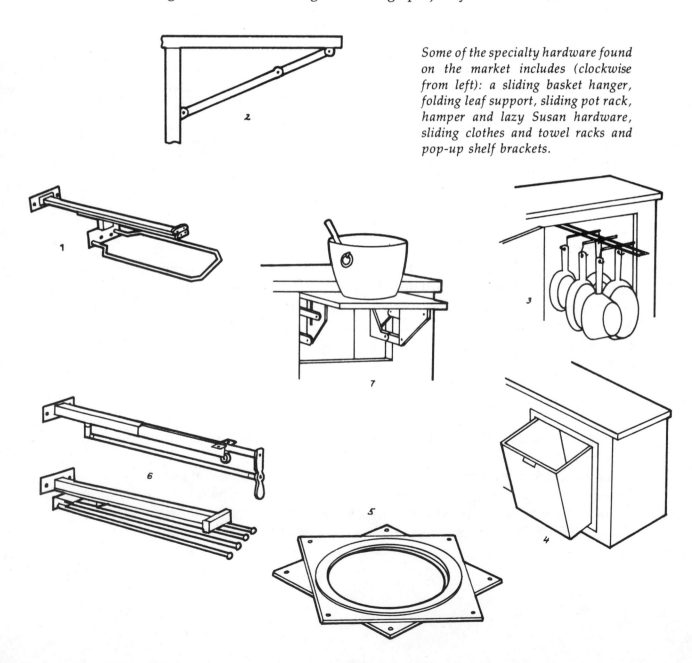

Some of the specialty hardware found on the market includes (clockwise from left): a sliding basket hanger, folding leaf support, sliding pot rack, hamper and lazy Susan hardware, sliding clothes and towel racks and pop-up shelf brackets.

EIGHT

Storage Projects and Variations

YOU CAN PURCHASE MANY ALREADY-MADE STORAGE units and they will serve your purposes quite well. However, all of them tend to be standardized, so you will have to make do with whatever sizes and shapes you can find.

You can also hire a cabinetmaker or carpenter to make units to fit your exact specifications. The work done by an individual pro will most likely be more expensive than buying mass-produced storage, but the work will fit your particular requirements. As a rule of thumb, a professional cabinetmaker will charge you between three and five times the cost of his materials. So if the cost of the wood and hardware is $100, the finished piece will run at least $300 and perhaps as much as $600. If you have the money, but neither the time, the tools nor the inclination to build the project yourself, then hire someone. But if it takes him 20 hours to build the project and you earn $10 an hour, you will have to be at your job for 30 hours before you have earned the cost of your storage. Is it worth it to work longer at your job than the carpenter does (or you would yourself), to have the piece built for you?

You will also pay a premium if you ask a professional to create a specialty item such as on-end drawers, double cabinets, a unique room divider or anything he has never made before. Professional carpenters earn their best living when the work they have to do is repetitious. If they can cut all the pieces for six identical cabinets at once, they can produce the six cabinets in about the same amount of time required to construct one uniquely designed box that demands that every piece be cut and joined to order. The professional will charge you proportionately more for the oddball item than he would for standard pieces, but will lose some of his earning power in the process because there is a limit to just how much he can charge. If he can earn $15 an hour doing straight, rough carpentry, but it takes him 60 hours to build your one-of-a-kind dish cabinet, will you really pay him $900? Probably not.

The principles of design and construction behind the storage ideas on the following pages are the same. The rabbet, dado and butt joints are always made in the same fashion, and should always be glued and then nailed or screwed together. The lumber should always be cut precisely. The process of sanding should always begin with a coarse grit and proceed to medium, fine and ultimately superfine. You should measure every distance at least three times, and allow ⅛" of wood for the width of your saw blade. Your nails should, as often as possible, be driven into the wood at angles. These are some of the rigid rules of carpentry that must be followed if your end product is to be stable and professional-looking, and strong enough to serve your storage needs.

The specific length and width, height and depth of each project are rarely identical to the dimensions of any other storage. A dead corner between two doorways can measure anywhere from 3' square to 3" in one direction and 2" in the other. Consequently, there is not much value in providing specific dimensions for every project shown on the following pages. Dimensions are included for such generic structures as standard kitchen cabinets and basic bookshelves, but even these are subject to the space you have to work with; they are meant as guideposts only.

These projects are offered as suggestions to stimulate your thinking. You should approach them as *ideas*. You may discover that what you see is exactly what you need and can build; you may also find that by combining two or more different ideas into the same unit, you can better solve your particular storage problems. If that's the case, pick and choose—take a piece of something here and an element of something else there, and redesign it to fit into the cubic space you have to work with. And when you have designed and built the storage you need—and it works—you will be amazed at how good you feel about having done all of the work yourself.

KITCHEN STORAGE

The most storage found in any single room in your home is in the kitchen. You can almost say that a kitchen is really one huge closet in which you keep utensils, food and food-preparation implements. Moreover, everything you store in your kitchen tends to be different in size and shape from practically everything else in the room, ranging from linen, silverware, boxes, cans, cleaning materials and tools to large and small appliances. To contain and make readily available all of these objects, a kitchen requires a huge variety of storage space, with almost as many different designs as there are objects.

Over the years cabinetmakers have, for their own purposes, standardized the dimensions of both under-the-counter and over-the-

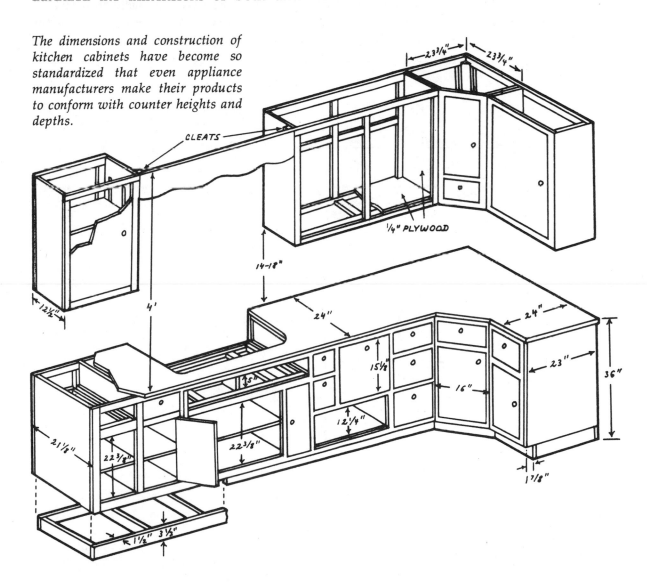

The dimensions and construction of kitchen cabinets have become so standardized that even appliance manufacturers make their products to conform with counter heights and depths.

counter storage. Only recently have they made any real concession to the people who use that storage, by inserting shelf tracks inside their cabinets so that shelves can be raised or lowered. Even this accommodation is a little shady since it is infinitely easier and quicker to nail tracks against a cabinet wall than it is to dado the sides for fixed shelves.

Counter Cabinets

The cabinets you find in most kitchens are mass-produced according to the dimensions given here, give or take an inch in any direction, and are almost always constructed in the manner shown. You can probably think of numerous ways to customize the basic storage area so that each cabinet serves your purposes more exactly. Some of the ways you can accomplish this customizing are suggested on the following pages.

The idea of a vertical drawer can be applied to almost any storage. The drawers themselves can be made to fit inside any under-the-counter cabinet.

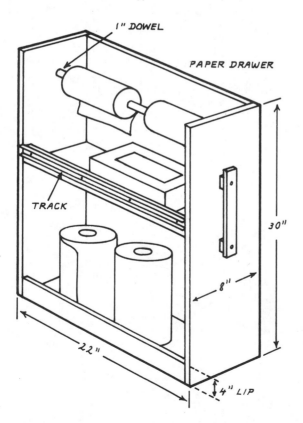

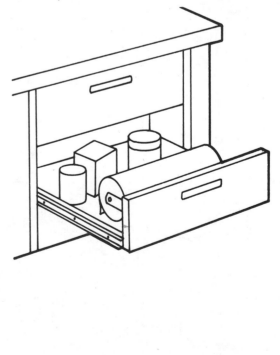

Two ways of holding waste bins in a vertical drawer.

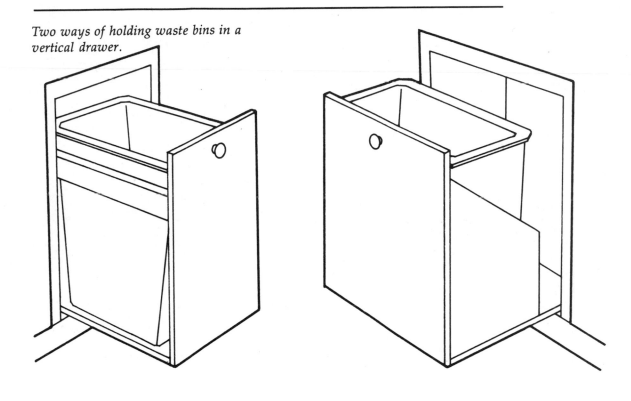

Alternatives for storing pot and pan lids.

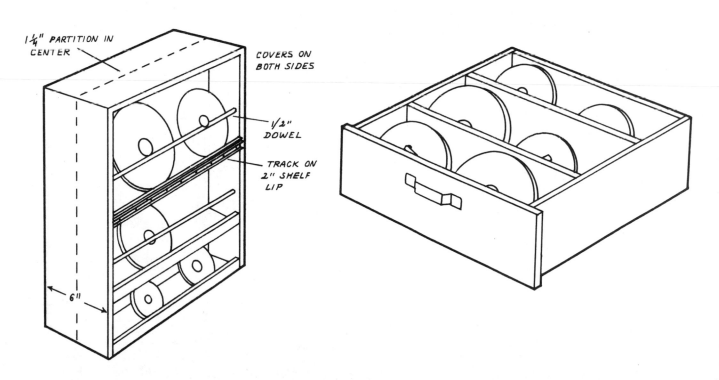

1 $\frac{1}{4}$" PARTITION IN CENTER

COVERS ON BOTH SIDES

1/2" DOWEL

TRACK ON 2" SHELF LIP

6"

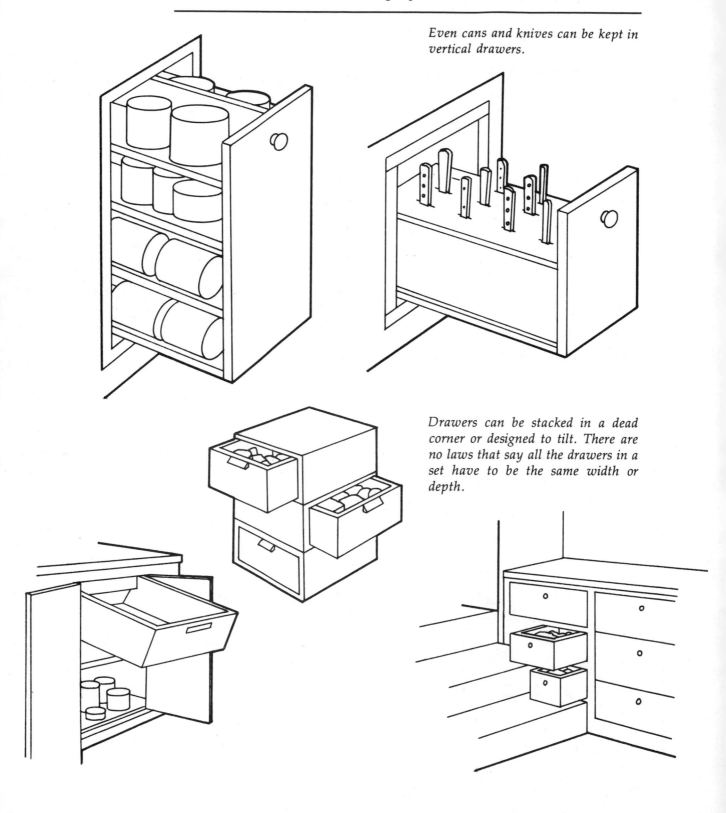

Even cans and knives can be kept in vertical drawers.

Drawers can be stacked in a dead corner or designed to tilt. There are no laws that say all the drawers in a set have to be the same width or depth.

Particularly in a kitchen, there are great advantages in buying ready-made wire baskets or plastic bins as storage drawers for vegetables and fruit.

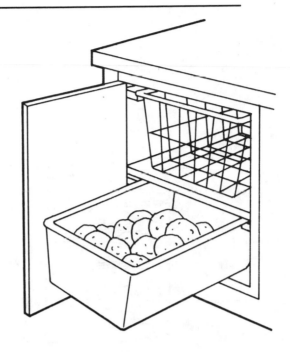

Drawers do not have to have sides or fronts that hide their contents; they can be trays that allow you to see what they are holding without pulling them out.

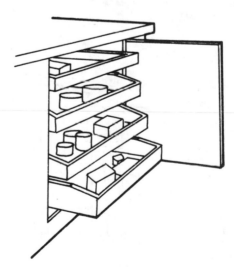

One of the ways you can make a standard kitchen cabinet more useful is to divide it into shelves that will hold specific objects such as baking tins, trays and pots.

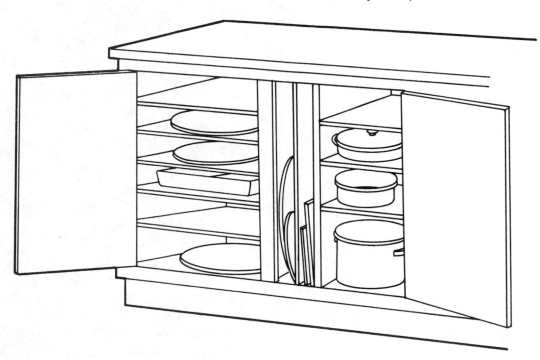

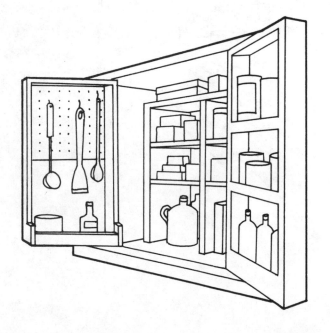

One of the most annoying spaces found in a kitchen is under a cooktop stove—it tends to be large, deep and inaccessible unless you organize it into compartments that will hold cookware, cleaning materials or dry goods. You can also store things on the double cabinet doors, either on hooks or by attaching a set of shelves.

Shelves do not have to be solid pieces of leveled wood. They can be tilted so that cans, for example, will roll toward the low end. Or the shelf might consist of two slotted and beveled strips of wood so that dishes can drain after they are washed.

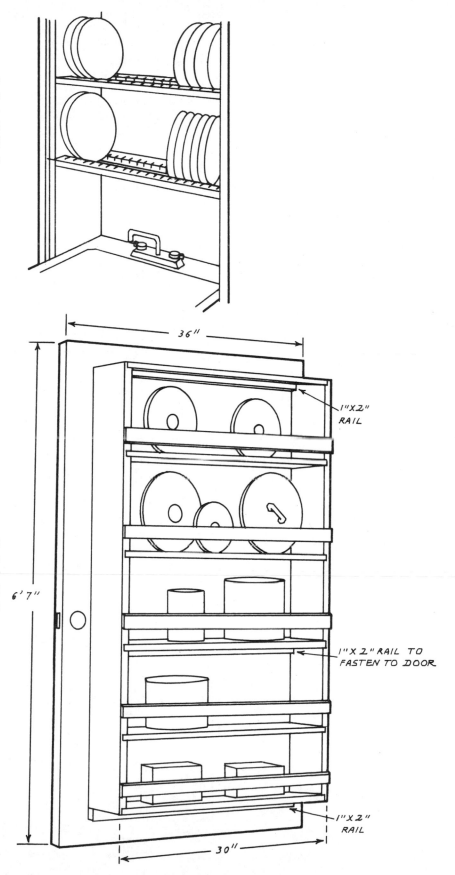

The construction of shelves to be hung on a door is basically the same no matter how large or small the door may be. Allow enough space around the shelves so that the door can open and close.

36"

1"X2" RAIL

6' 7"

1"X2" RAIL TO FASTEN TO DOOR

1"X2" RAIL

30"

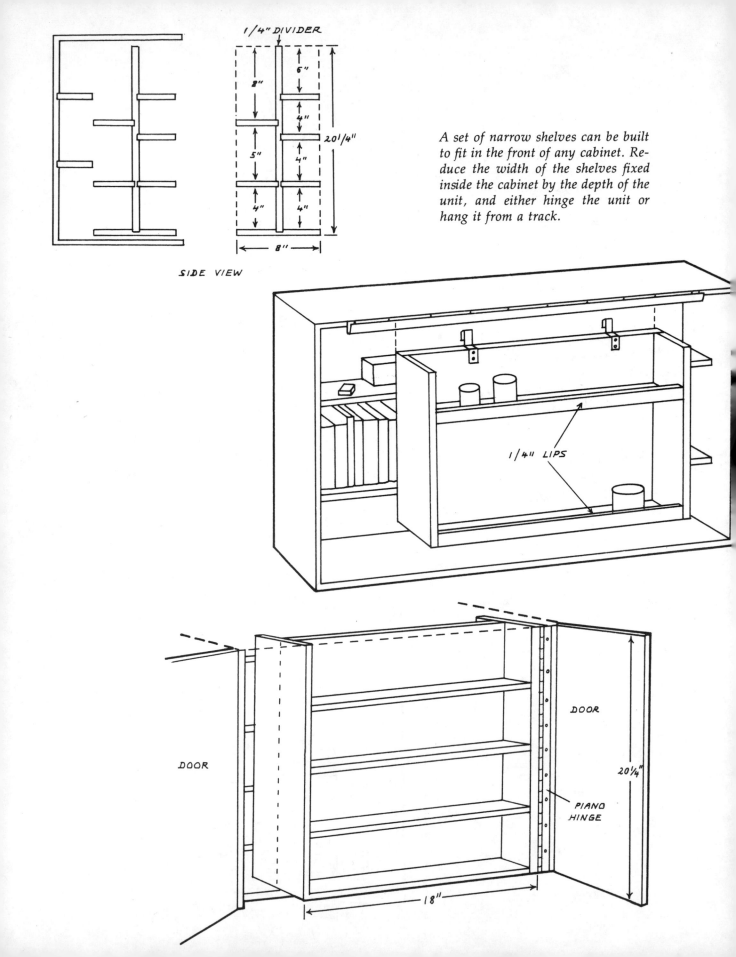

1/4" DIVIDER

6"

2"

4"

4"

20 1/4"

5"

4"

4"

8"

SIDE VIEW

A set of narrow shelves can be built to fit in the front of any cabinet. Reduce the width of the shelves fixed inside the cabinet by the depth of the unit, and either hinge the unit or hang it from a track.

1/4" LIPS

DOOR

DOOR

20 1/4"

PIANO HINGE

18"

Construction plans for a lazy Susan corner cabinet. The lazy Susan can be completely round, in which case its door must be a half round or a sliding tambour. Usually a notch is cut out of one side of the Susan to hold the cabinet facing.

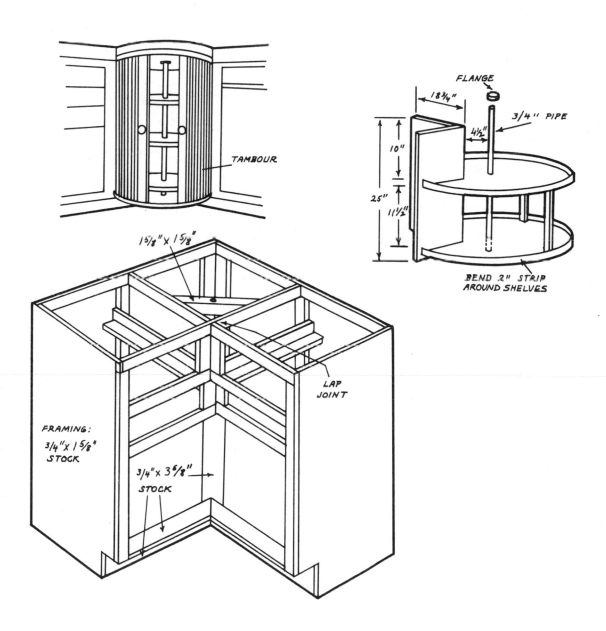

FLANGE

18¾"

3/4" PIPE

4½"

10"

25"

11½"

BEND 2" STRIP
AROUND SHELVES

TAMBOUR

1⅝" X 1⅝"

LAP
JOINT

FRAMING:
3/4" X 1⅝"
STOCK

3/4" X 3⅝"
STOCK

Bins and hampers can be employed to hold things such as sugar and flour. The bins themselves ought to be made of tin and can be purchased at some hardware stores and many specialty shops. But you can also make them out of hardboard and plywood.

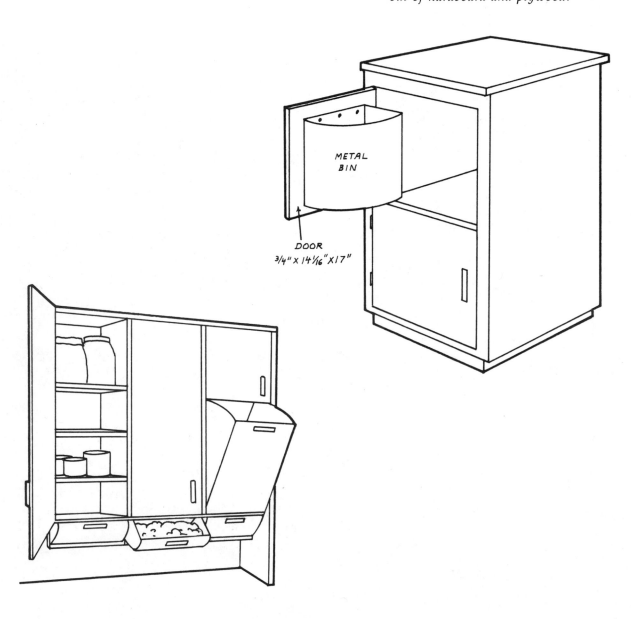

METAL
BIN

DOOR
3/4" X 14 1/16" X 17"

There are a lot of ways to hang or store pots and pans (A). Narrow vertical slots are always useful (B). You can store knives by cutting a slot in the front of a wide shelf lip (C). The knives will stay in place better if you also attach a strip magnet to the bottom of the shelf above the blades. As for all those spice jars you can never find enough shelf space for, nail the tops to a rotating block of 2"×2" wood that can span the center of a cabinet (D). The wood is held between the cabinet walls by driving screws into its ends.

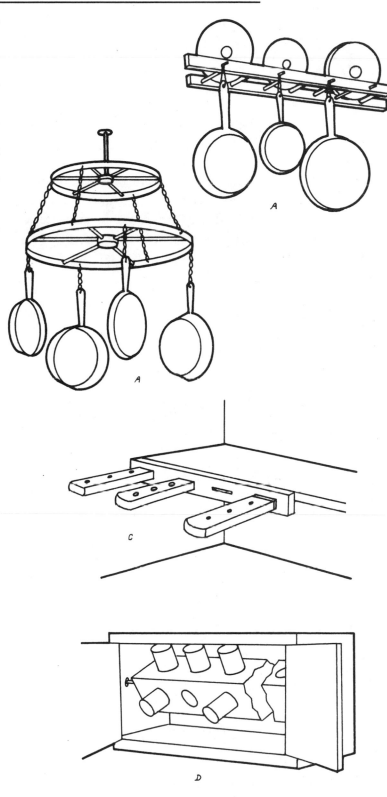

A

A

C

D

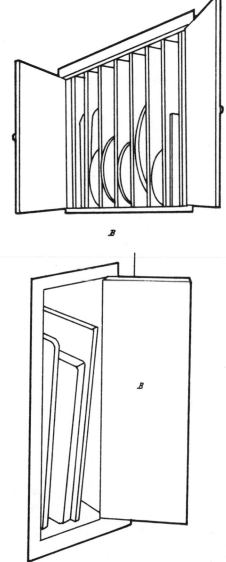

B

B

Added Kitchen Storage

When you have finished reappointing the stock cabinets under and over your kitchen counters, there may still be a need for more storage in your kitchen. You have several alternatives, depending on how much space is left in the room. Generally you want to leave at least 3' of walking area in front of every counter and storage unit; 4' is better. The rest of the floor area can be taken up with storage islands, peninsulas or towers, and any leftover wall space can be used for pantries. Here are a few versions of each, but bear in mind that each of these units is essentially a box which can have its interior space divided and arranged in any manner that suits your purposes. It can include shelves, cabinets, drawers or other useful divisions.

The vertical drawer idea can get to be 7' or 8' high, at which point it must pull out of its slot on wheels. The drawer can be as narrow or wide as the space you have for it and can hold all kinds of objects.

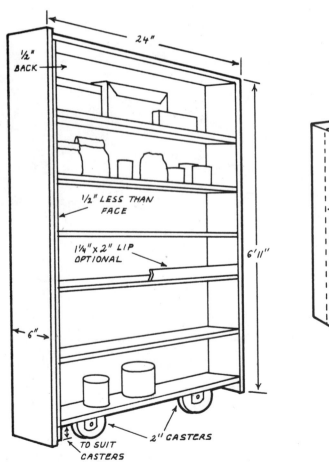

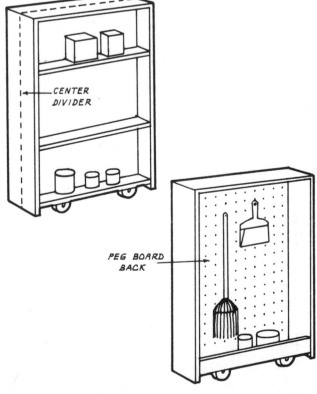

Shelves can go practically anywhere.
They can fill up the walls of a walk-
in closet, or be narrow enough (3½″)
to hide behind an open kitchen door,
where they will hold your canned
goods.

Some ways of arranging shelves around bulky objects.

Construction of a corner cabinet. If the width of the door is more than 18", its weight will make it sag unless a caster is attached under the leading edge.

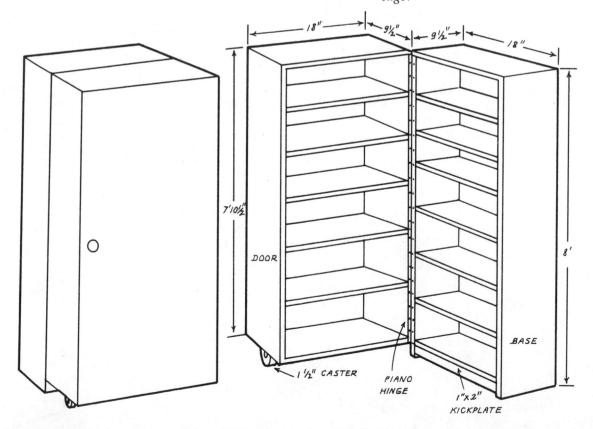

18"

9½"

9½"

18"

7'10½"

8'

DOOR

BASE

1½" CASTER

PIANO HINGE

1"x2" KICKPLATE

If the corner is big enough, attach two shelf doors to the sides of a shelf tower. Or you can have swinging shelves in the front of a small closet and hide them with the closet door.

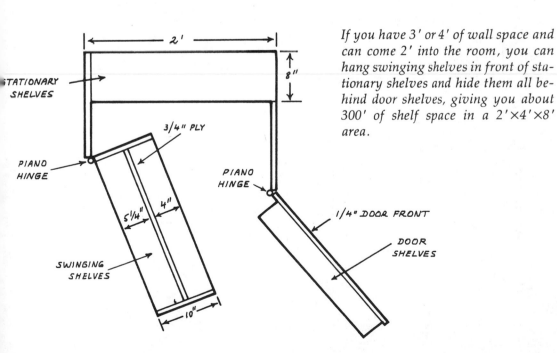

If you have 3' or 4' of wall space and can come 2' into the room, you can hang swinging shelves in front of stationary shelves and hide them all behind door shelves, giving you about 300' of shelf space in a 2'×4'×8' area.

Peninsulas traditionally extend at right angles into the room and provide a counter top as well as storage space, but you can skip the counter part and use them as a room divider full of storage.

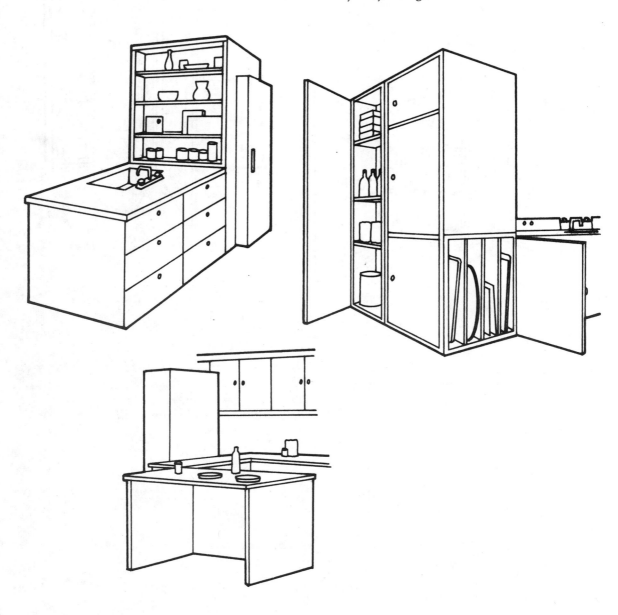

Islands can assume any shape or size, can be designed to wash at, eat from or cook on, as well as to store things.

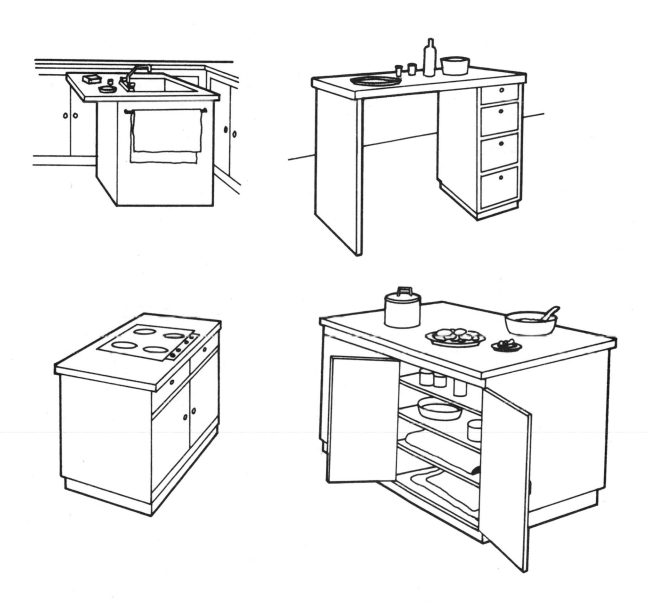

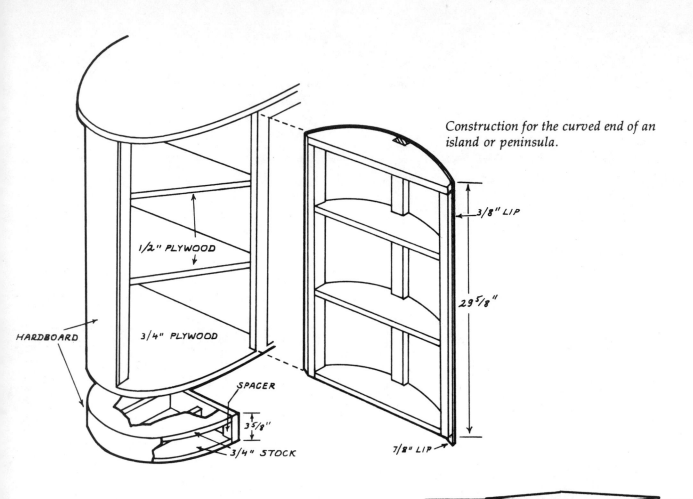

HARDBOARD

1/2" PLYWOOD

3/4" PLYWOOD

SPACER

3 5/8"

3/4" STOCK

Construction for the curved end of an island or peninsula.

3/8" LIP

29 5/8"

7/8" LIP

If an island is too high to be used as a counter, it becomes a storage tower. You can put anything in a tower and get to it from any direction. Not only can a tower have shelves, hooks, dividers, drawers and cabinets, but it could also hold an oven and/or refrigerator or a stackable clothes washer and dryer.

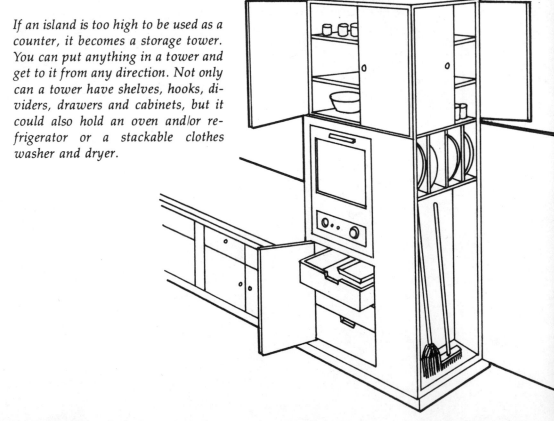

BATHROOMS

Relatively speaking, bathrooms contain almost as large a variety of objects as kitchens. Bathrooms are liable to hold anything from linens, towels and dirty laundry to cosmetics, hair dryers, scales, cleaning equipment and other sundries used in our daily lives. The major problem is that most contractors build the bathroom into the smallest possible area. Consequently, there is rarely much space to store all of those bathroom things—usually only part of a wall or two, the ceiling and under the sink.

The sink in a small bathroom is a frustrating object to a storage seeker. There it is, hung from the wall, offering itself as the top of about 4 cubic feet of juicy storage area—except there is a whole tangle of water pipes cutting right into the middle of the space. You can purchase or build a vanity to fit under or even around a sink, but all that gives you is a storage box. You then must be very artful about hanging shelves around those pipes.

Sink Stands

Sinks, being what they are, all come in pretty much the same dimensions; and plumbers, being what they are, hang all sinks pretty much the same distance from the floor. But depending on where the sink is located and whether it is supported by a vanity or hung directly on the wall, there is considerable leeway for developing workable storage, beginning with the basic dimensions of the vanity itself.

More Bathroom Storage

If you have a free wall in your bathroom, you can go for a whole wall unit and make it as intricate and complete a storage center as the space allows. Given less wall space, particularly in bathrooms where half the height of the wall is covered by tiles, you are reduced to hanging a variety of cabinets from the wall above the tiles.

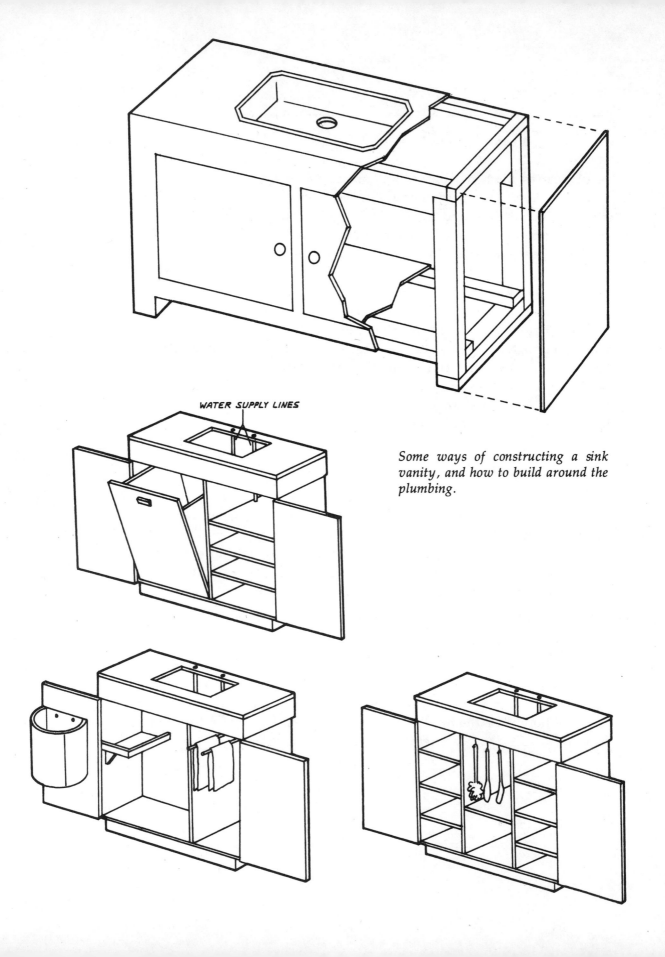

WATER SUPPLY LINES

Some ways of constructing a sink vanity, and how to build around the plumbing.

All hamper construction is basically the same, but the sides and backs may have to be notched to get around the sink drainpipe.

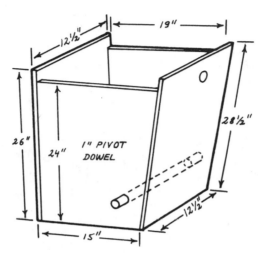

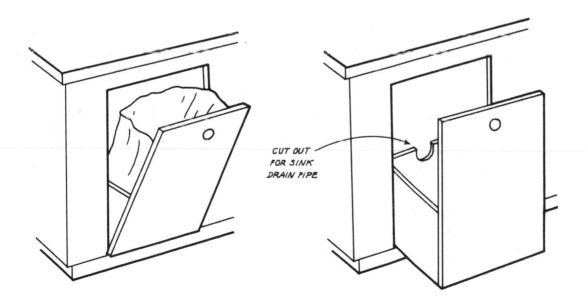

CUT OUT
FOR SINK
DRAIN PIPE

With most bathrooms you have to think in terms of tight space, but there are all kinds of ways to fill the nooks and crannies with shelves, drawers and cabinets, as well as with hooks and towel bars.

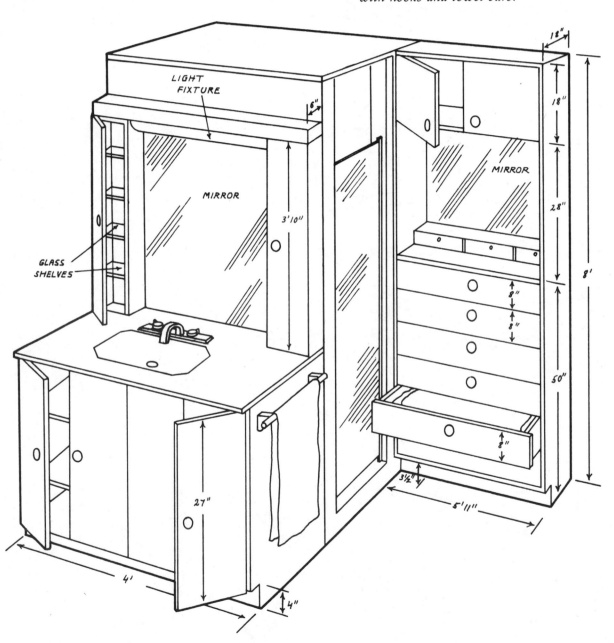

Above a toilet there is almost always dead wall space and often a corner as well. Here are a couple of ways you can use the space for storage.

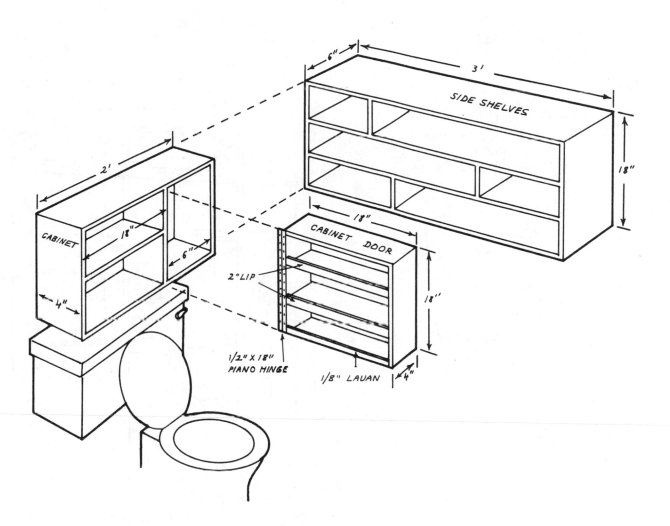

If cabinets are not necessary, you can literally surround most toilets with shelves and towel bars.

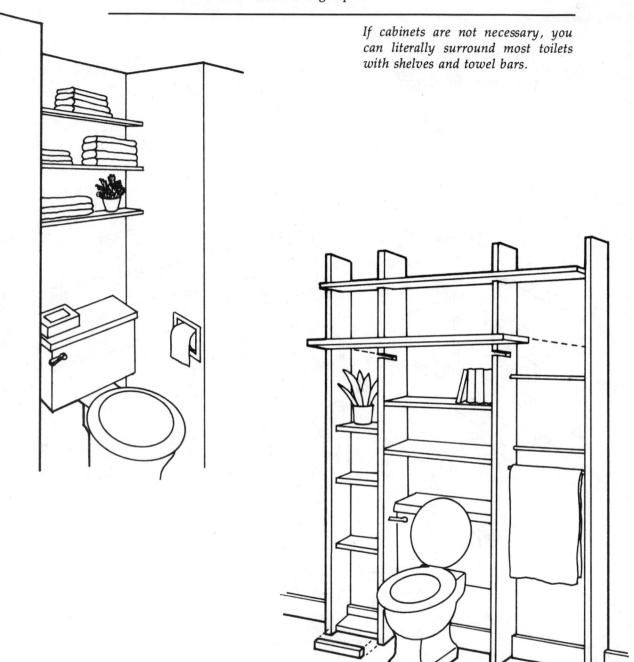

Small objects collect dust and ought
to be covered. A set of notions
shelves can be given a lipped cover
(A), or the shelves can have a back
and be hinged directly to the wall
(B). The best way to keep control
over such items as pill bottles and
cosmetics is to compartmentalize
them in either a cabinet or drawers (C).

LIVING CENTERS

Living rooms, family rooms, dining rooms and bedrooms usually offer considerable expanses of wall area that can be taken up with standing closets, shelves or room-high cabinets. You have more space to work with, but because everyone will see the fruits of your labors on a daily basis, you must spend more time and effort applying an attractive finish to whatever surfaces are on constant view.

Shelves

It is amazing how many ways you can hang a simple shelf, and how many different forms those shelves can take. The shelf need only be crosscut at the proper length. The real work comes when you begin developing a system of vertical supports to hold it in place. All the possibilities of making shelves stay in place could not be represented here.

The shelves in living areas usually should be decorative. The basic bookcase is always constructed in more or less the same way. It is the molding, trim and finish you add that give it the attractiveness you can live with day after day.

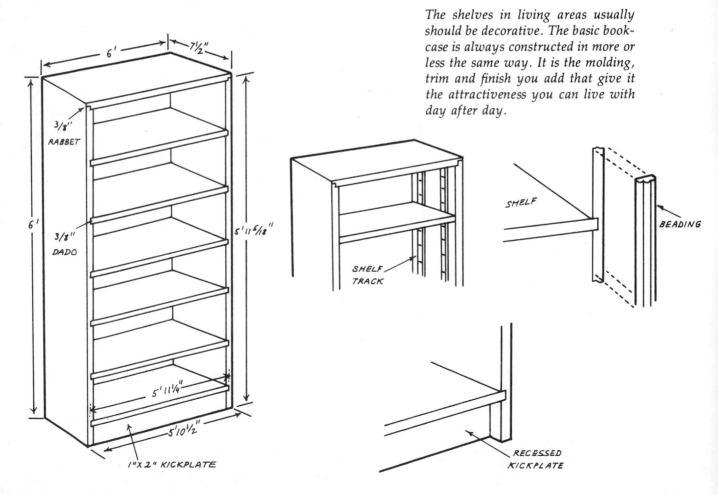

There is nothing like a set of folding shelves for storing toys. The dimensions given here will provide over 100' of shelving. The basic unit should be anchored to the wall, and both swing units must have casters.

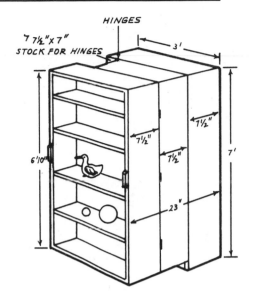

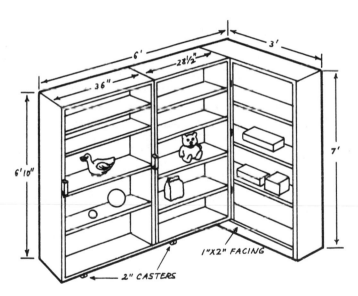

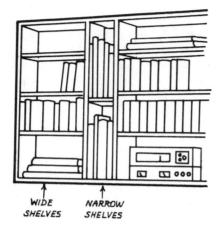

WIDE
SHELVES

NARROW
SHELVES

The shelves in a living area can be wide or very narrow, or even set on drawer guides, depending on their primary use.

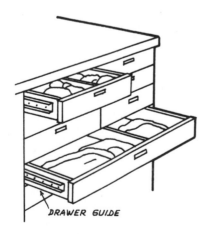

DRAWER GUIDE

To support a shelf, you can use almost anything that is strong and stable. A pair of ladders will do nicely in
a child's room or a tool shop. A
whole bookcase can be made out of
1"×2" stock. Sometimes a pair of ris-
ers can be used to support a tier of
small shelves held in place with
hanger straps.

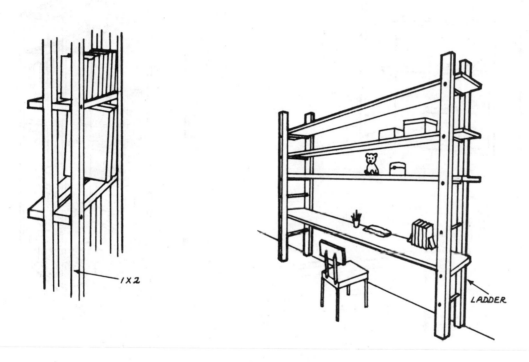

— 1 X 2

LADDER

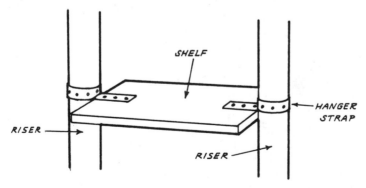

SHELF

HANGER
STRAP

RISER —

RISER

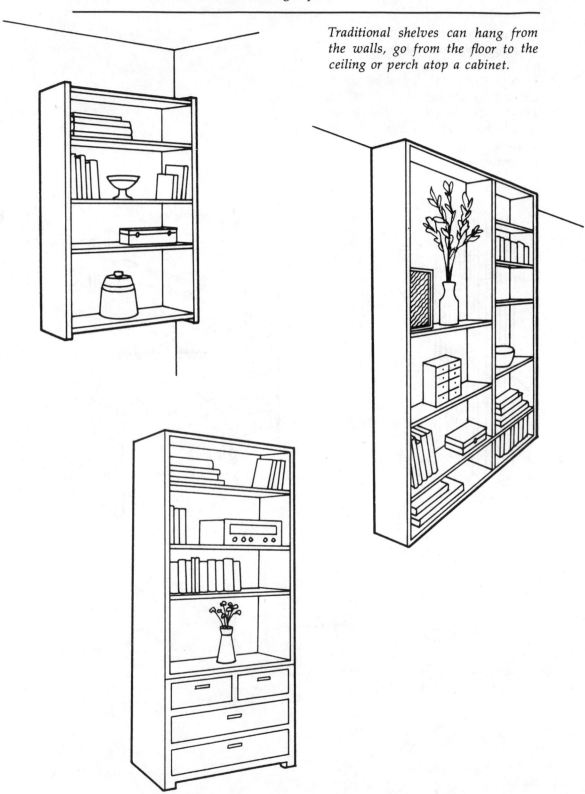

Traditional shelves can hang from the walls, go from the floor to the ceiling or perch atop a cabinet.

Shelves, like all other storage elements, should be designed for specific purposes. If you cut big notches out of a shelf, there is not much it can do except hold your hats (A). Given smaller notches and slots, you can hang your stemware upside down to keep dust out (B). You can also drill holes in a shelf to allow air to get at your glassware (C). Use perforated hardwoard to store laundry so that it will not become mildewed (D); if you divide the perforated shelf into sections, you can organize laundry according to the proper washer loads. You can attach a shelf to the rafters with a block-and-tackle system, using some of the airspace in your garage, attic or basement (E).

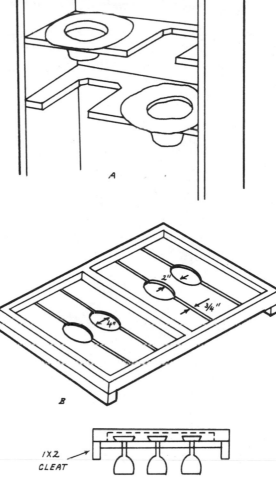

A

B

1X2
CLEAT

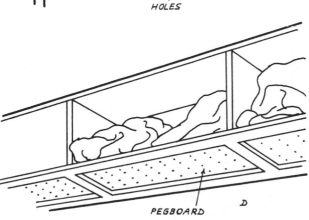

C

HOLES

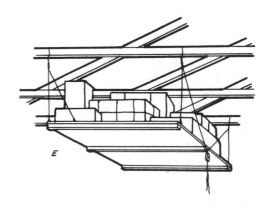

PEGBOARD   D

E

Cabinets

The basic cabinet is a box with a door on it. It can remain plain or become fancy with the addition of shelves or drawers and even cabinets inside the cabinet. You can make cabinets that stand on the floor or hang from the walls or ceilings. But no matter what you do with them or how they are designed, they are all still boxes.

Basic cabinet construction and a few variations.

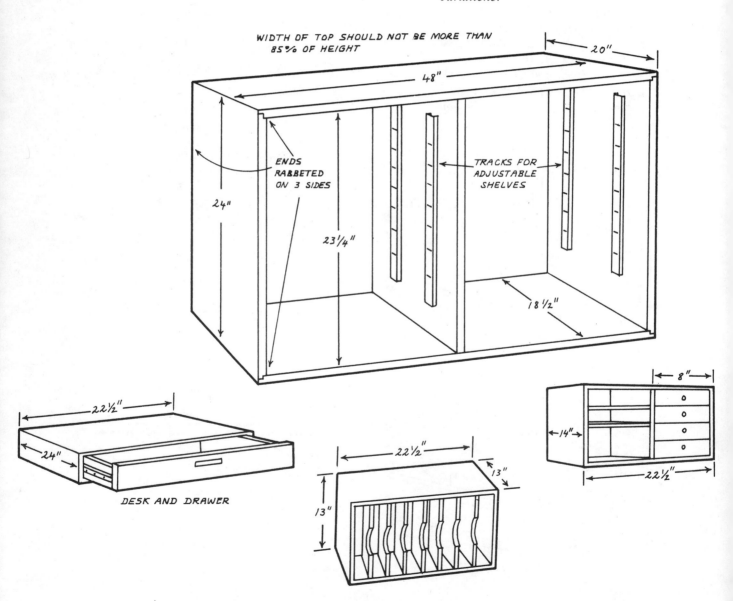

WIDTH OF TOP SHOULD NOT BE MORE THAN 85% OF HEIGHT

20"

48"

24"

ENDS RABBETED ON 3 SIDES

TRACKS FOR ADJUSTABLE SHELVES

23¼"

18½"

22½"

24"

DESK AND DRAWER

22½"

13"

13"

8"

14"

22½"

A plan for a cabinet with swinging storage units.

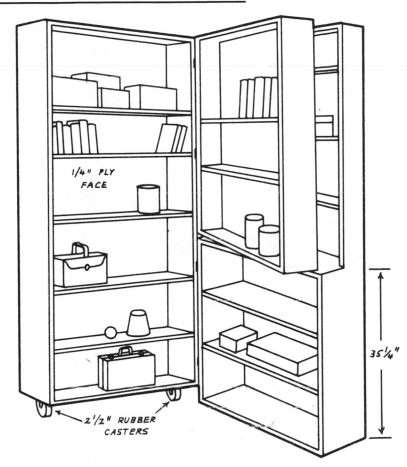

1/4" PLY
FACE

35¼"

2½" RUBBER
CASTERS

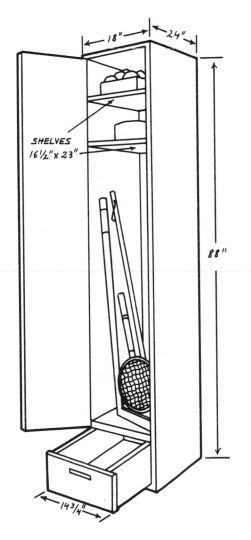

18"   24"

SHELVES
16½" x 23"

88"

14¾"

Narrow, deep cabinets are ideal for housing sports equipment as well as cleaning supplies and implements.

Cabinets with drawers and shelves can be squeezed into almost any available space.

You can take advantage of a relatively useless small window by using it as the light source for a whole complex of built-in cabinets and shelves.

Dividers

When cabinets and shelves get to be so large they stick far into the room, you can begin to use them as room dividers, making them a wall unto themselves. Again, there are infinite designs and arrangements incorporating everything from bookshelves to a desk, cabinets for files to drawers for stereo and television equipment. It is probably best to first decide just how long and how high you want your room divider to be in terms of how its presence will affect the room you are dividing. Then begin to separate your divider into the specific components you need for storage.

Room dividers can be less than waist high and just wide enough to hold books, plants or glassware.

A room divider can also be ceiling high and thick enough to provide storage on both sides. The elements that comprise a full room divider depend strictly on what is being stored.

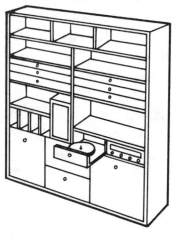

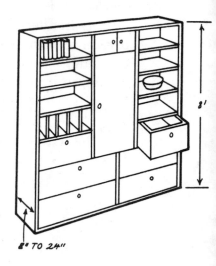

8'

8" TO 24"

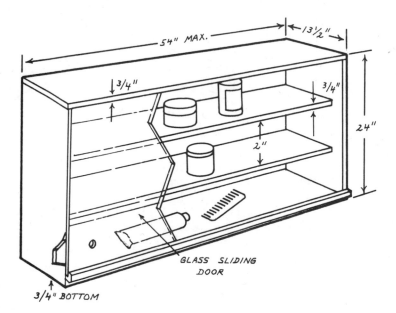

54" MAX.

13½"

¾"

¾"

24"

2"

GLASS SLIDING DOOR

¾" BOTTOM

Another way of dividing a room is to hang a cabinet over a counter. The cabinet can have solid, hinged doors, but glass sliding doors create the effect of leaving the space open even though it has been divided.

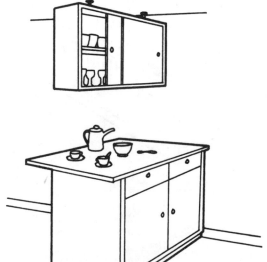

WORK AREAS

Work areas, whether they are for gardening, sewing or building things, must always contain a table or bench, room for the worker to move about in and endless storage space. The storage can be most efficient if it hangs from the joists, which are often uncovered in basements, garages or attics (where they are called rafters if they hold the roof over the house). The workbench, which is really just a big shelf, should be designed to the exact specifications of the user and be given absolute preference to everything else in the room. However your bench design ends up, you are bound to have plenty of space for storing things under, behind, beside and above it. How that storage is devised is up to you, but here are some suggested approaches to an orderly work area. You may be able to combine elements to suit the activities that will go on in your work room.

Construction drawing for assembling a workbench.

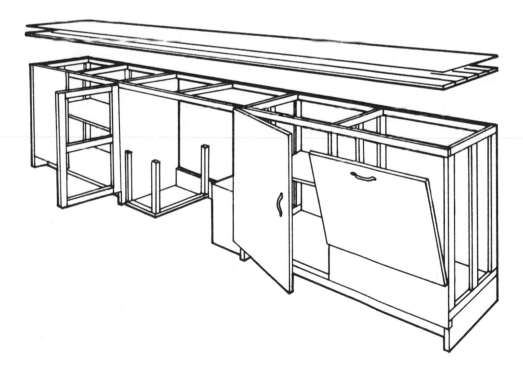

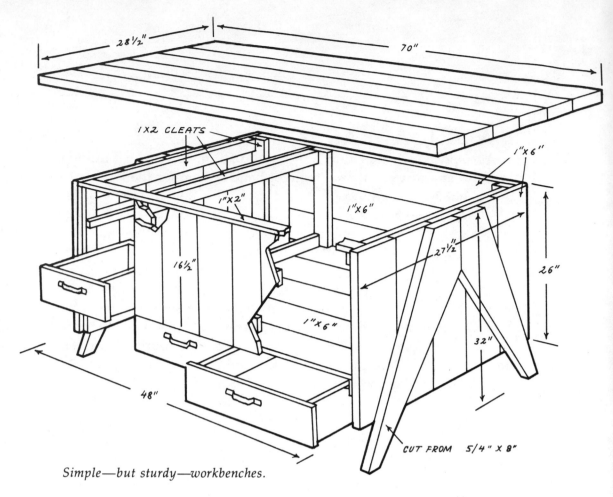

28½"   70"

1X2 CLEATS

1"X6"

1"X2"

1"X6"

16½"

27½"

26"

1"X6"

32"

48"

CUT FROM 5/4" X 8"

Simple—but sturdy—workbenches.

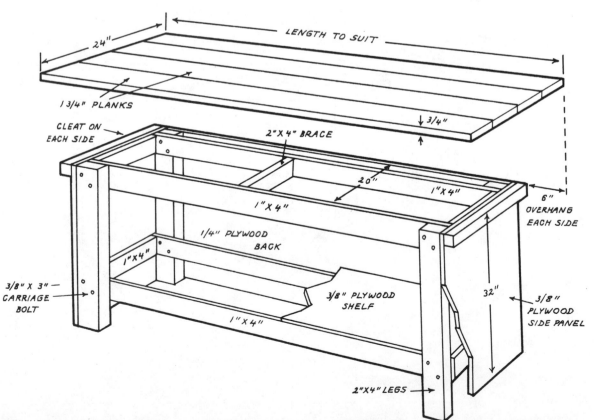

24"   LENGTH TO SUIT

1 3/4" PLANKS

3/4"

CLEAT ON EACH SIDE

2"X 4" BRACE

20"

1"X 4"

1"X 4"

6" OVERHANG EACH SIDE

1/4" PLYWOOD BACK

1"X 4"

32"

3/8" X 3" CARRIAGE BOLT

3/8" PLYWOOD SHELF

3/8" PLYWOOD SIDE PANEL

1"X 4"

2"X4" LEGS

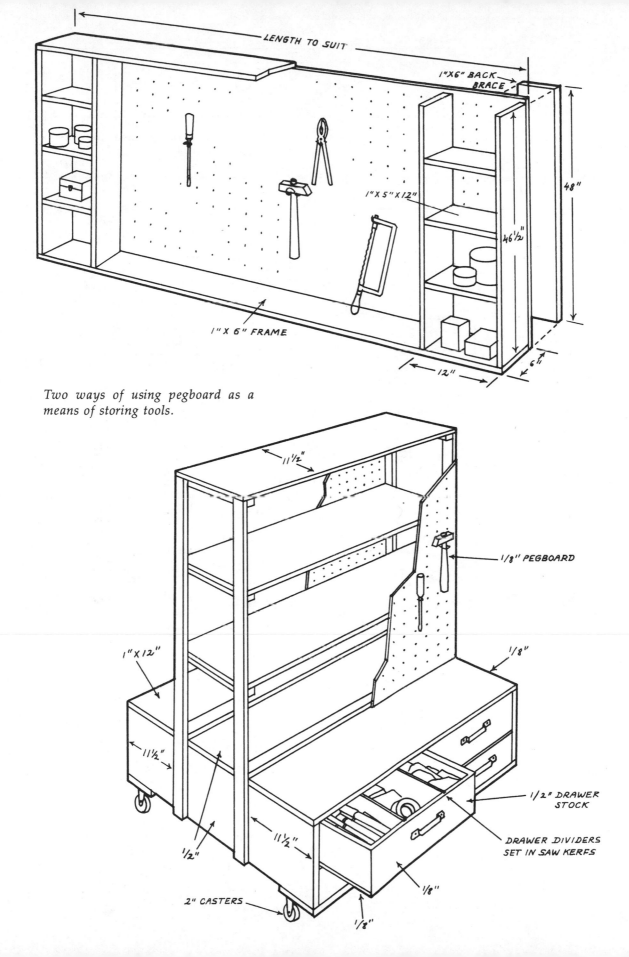

LENGTH TO SUIT

1"X6" BACK BRACE

48"

1"X 5"X 12"

46½"

1" X 6" FRAME

12"

6"

Two ways of using pegboard as a means of storing tools.

11½"

1/8" PEGBOARD

1"X 12"

1/8"

11½"

1/2" DRAWER STOCK

DRAWER DIVIDERS SET IN SAW KERFS

11½"

1/2"

1/8"

2" CASTERS

1/8"

Basic toolshed construction, using exterior-grade plywood.

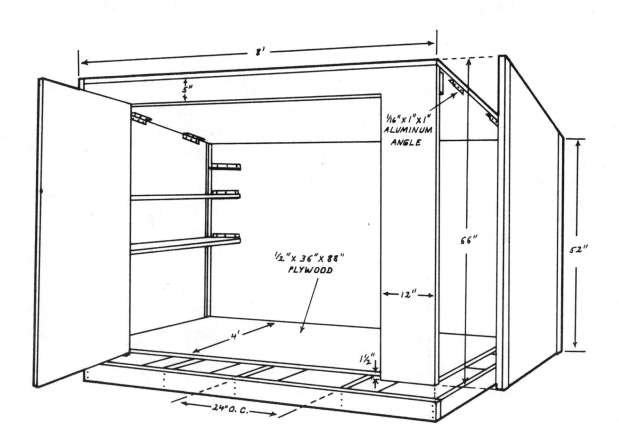

A potting bench can usually take advantage of hampers and rolling bins, but it also needs specialized storage units to hold such odd-shaped tools as rakes and shovels.

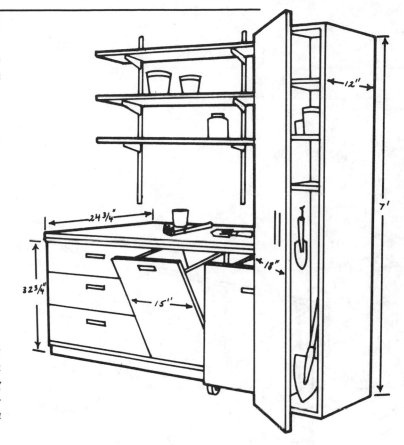

The work space around laundry equipment should be ample enough to facilitate folding and stacking clothing. As a result, there are usually more shelves than cabinets in a laundry area.

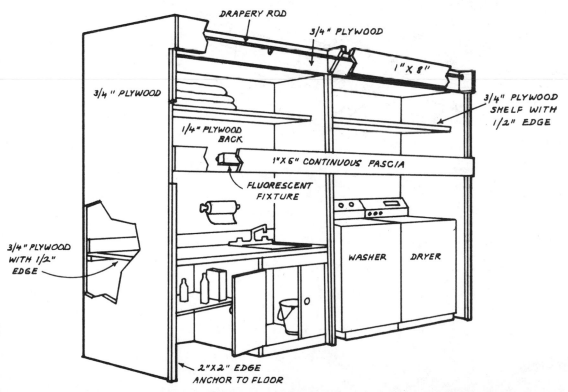

Study areas need be no larger than a desk top, which in this case is 18"×36". But whether the desk hangs from a wall, is built into the corner of a room or is part of a room divider, there should be enough shelves for books, at least one drawer and perhaps a cabinet.

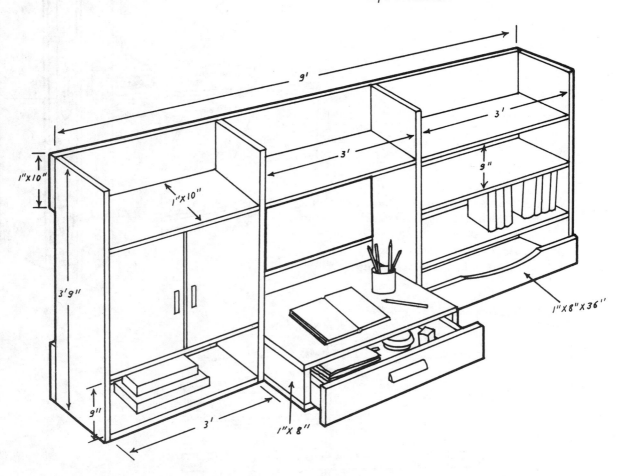

Three of the endless number of study-area arrangements.

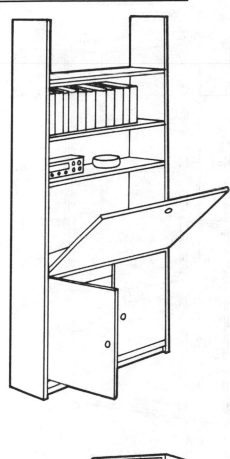

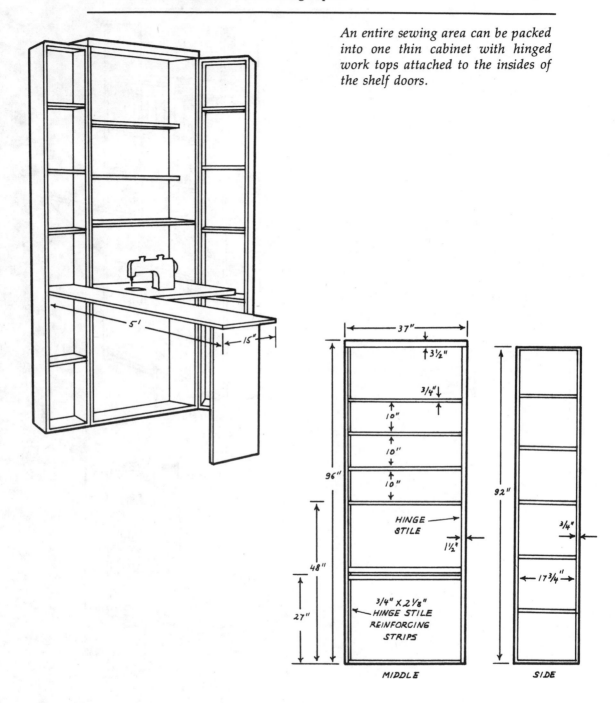

An entire sewing area can be packed into one thin cabinet with hinged work tops attached to the insides of the shelf doors.

5'

15"

37"

3½"

¾"

10"

10"

10"

HINGE
STILE

1½"

96"

48"

27"

¾" X 2⅛"
HINGE STILE
REINFORCING
STRIPS

MIDDLE

92"

¾"

17¾"

SIDE

Storing sewing supplies requires a considerable number of small storage units such as (clockwise) clear plastic bins (A), pegboards (B), magazine rack arrangements (C), and even finishing nails hammered into a slanted board to hold spools of thread (D).

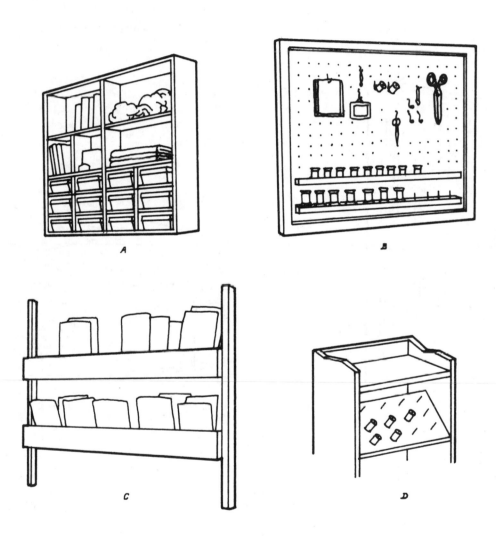

A

B

C

D

CLOSETS

When a cabinet gets big enough to stand in, you have a closet. Closets are normally buried in the walls of your home and, as any adult knows, there are never enough of them. A basic closet can be created by building a wall or two and inserting a door. But there are some really ingenious ways of rearranging the insides of all the closets you already have so that you can get more things inside them. There are also some odd-sized triangular holes in your home that can be converted into useful closet space.

Into every closet there may go any manner of storage elements. Each article of clothing should have a specific place.

Under-the-Something Storage

There are two places in most homes that offer natural out-of-the-way storage space. The trouble is, if you store anything in them, it will have to be retrieved by lying on your stomach and reaching as far as you can into a dark corner. With triangles, as with any other hard-to-reach spaces, the solution becomes a matter of bringing the storage out to you, where it is convenient to get at whatever you have put there. This means using wheels and/or tracks so that you can have drawers or rolling bins that will snuggle discreetly against the angle of a roof or the underside of a stairway, then be pulled out to meet you. The variations of this pull-out principle are infinite.

Frame construction for an under-the-stairs closet that is ideal for storing seasonal sports equipment or tools.

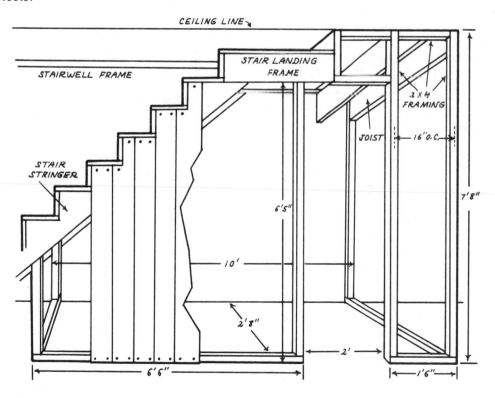

CEILING LINE

STAIR LANDING FRAME

STAIRWELL FRAME

2 X 4 FRAMING

JOIST   16" O.C.

STAIR STRINGER

6'5"

7'8"

10'

2'8"

2'

6'6"

1'6"

Some ways of getting the most out of triangular storage space. The design of roll-out bins or shelves is dictated by the objects being stored.

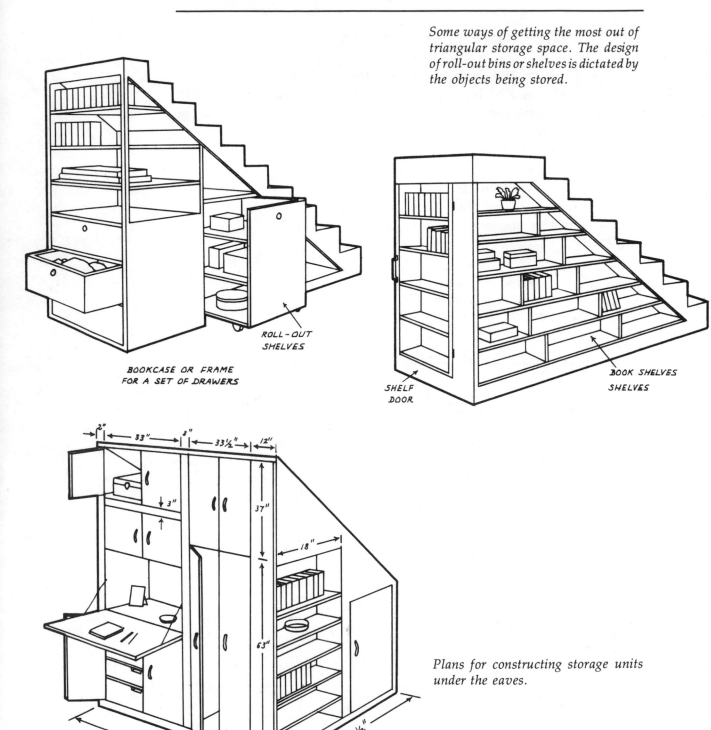

BOOKCASE OR FRAME
FOR A SET OF DRAWERS

ROLL-OUT
SHELVES

SHELF
DOOR

BOOK SHELVES
SHELVES

Plans for constructing storage units under the eaves.

Special Closets

You can have special closets to hold your linens, dishes or tools. These are usually narrow shelves that are accessible by opening a door. But when they are the size of a clothes closet, they present a full range of possibilities for hanging and storing things. Never hesitate to go right to the ceiling, either. A wide shelf 8' above the floor may not be easy to reach, but it is a great place for keeping all that luggage you use only about four times a year. Some of the ways you can rearrange your closet space are suggested here.

Basic stud and drywall construction. The studs around the door should be doubled; corners require three 2×4s. Closets can be made with 2"×3" stock, and if the drywall is ⅝" thick, you can get away with placing the studs 24" on center.

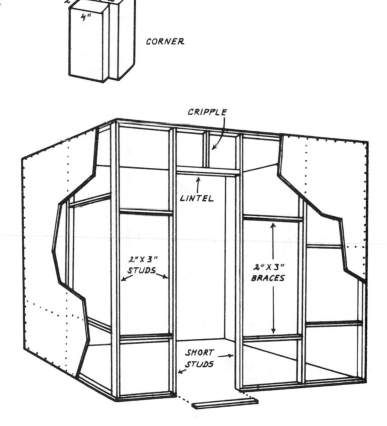

Bins and boxes are excellent organizers for things like toys. Ties, jewelry and shoes can be hung from the backs of closet doors. Clear plastic drawers are ideal for storing shoes, hats and sweaters. You can hang trousers, but you can also build a set of 14"×48" sliding trays that are 3" deep and store your pants flat.

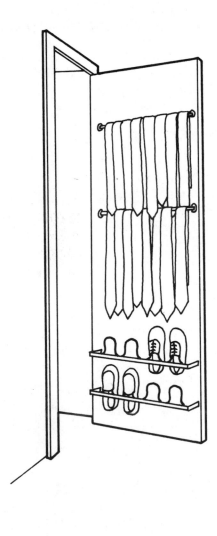

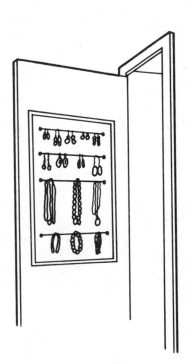

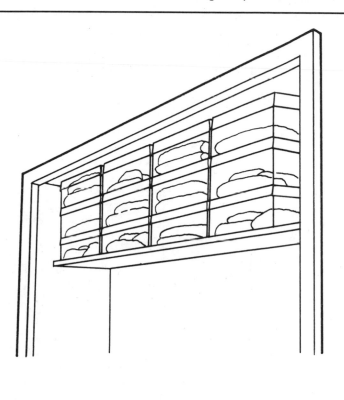

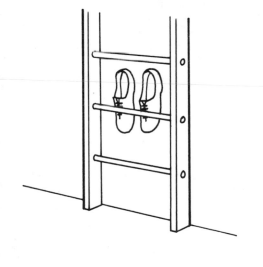

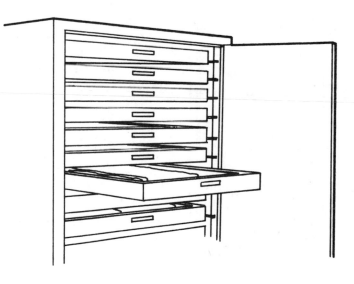

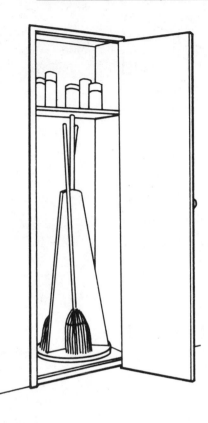

Other kinds of closets can use such elements as a lazy Susan, pegboard or special dividers for unusually shaped equipment.

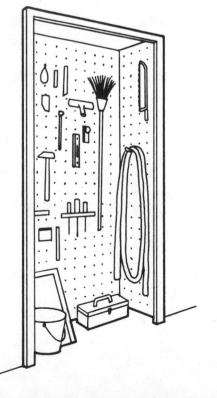

ODDS AND ENDS

In every home there are a host of odd-shaped possessions that need to be stored, but defy normal storage space. The solution is to build special places for keeping them.

Card tables, TV trays and folding chairs are clumsy objects to store unless you have a specific bin or hamper for them.

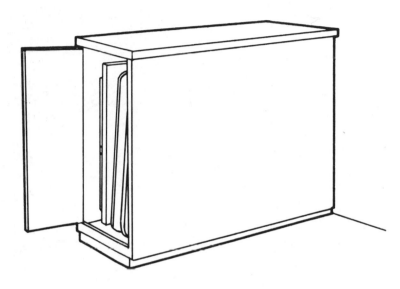

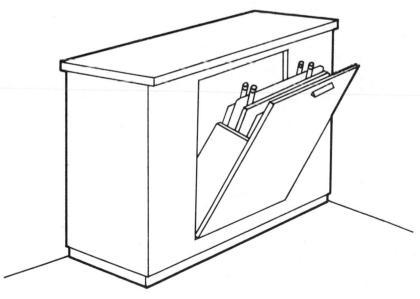

A simple rack made from 1"×2" stock can be extremely useful near an outside door or in a work area.

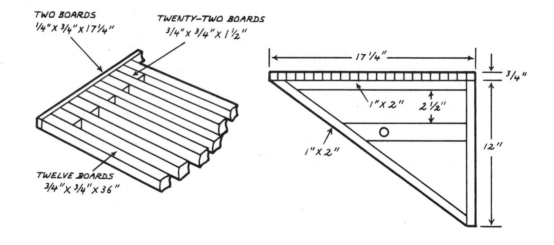

1" DOWEL

6"

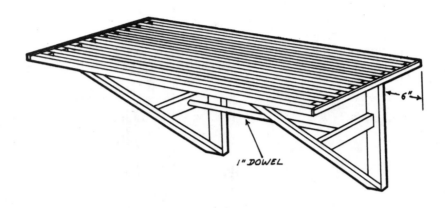

TWO BOARDS
1/4" x 3/4" x 17 1/4"

TWENTY-TWO BOARDS
3/4" x 3/4" x 1 1/2"

TWELVE BOARDS
3/4" x 3/4" x 36"

17 1/4"

3/4"

1" X 2"

2 1/2"

1" X 2"

12"

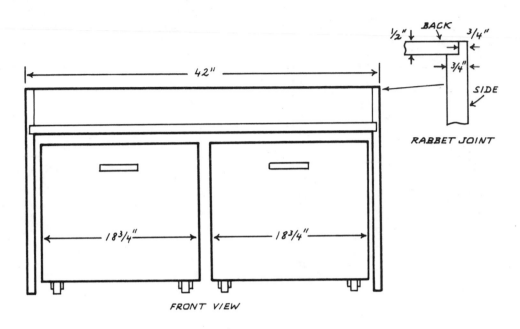

RABBET JOINT

FRONT VIEW

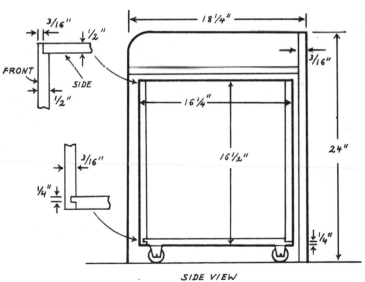

SIDE VIEW

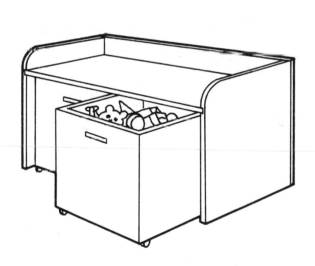

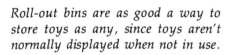

*Roll-out bins are as good a way to
store toys as any, since toys aren't
normally displayed when not in use.*

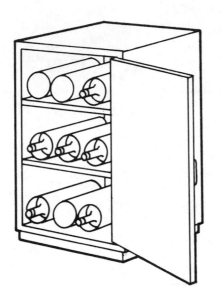

There are several ways of storing wine bottles, including putting each bottle in a cardboard mailing sleeve.

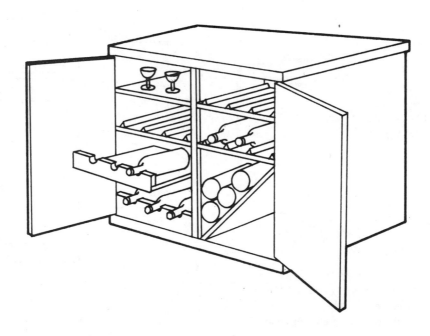

Radiators are not only unsightly, but they take up usable living space. Since utilizing the space immediately around a radiator is often difficult, you might as well turn it into storage. You must allow air to circulate around the radiator; the easiest way to do that is to build frame-and-panel doors with either perforated hardwood panels or decorative metal screening nailed to the backs of the frames. The housing around the radiator then becomes a support for shelves, a bench, a narrow bin for storing card and TV tables, or cabinets.

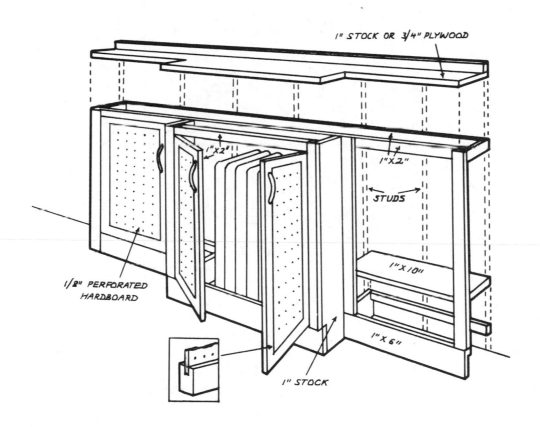

1" STOCK OR 3/4" PLYWOOD

1"X2"

1"X2"

STUDS

1"X10"

1/2" PERFORATED HARDBOARD

1"X6"

1" STOCK

Most sports equipment can be stored along the wall of a garage or basement in space that is no more than 12" deep.

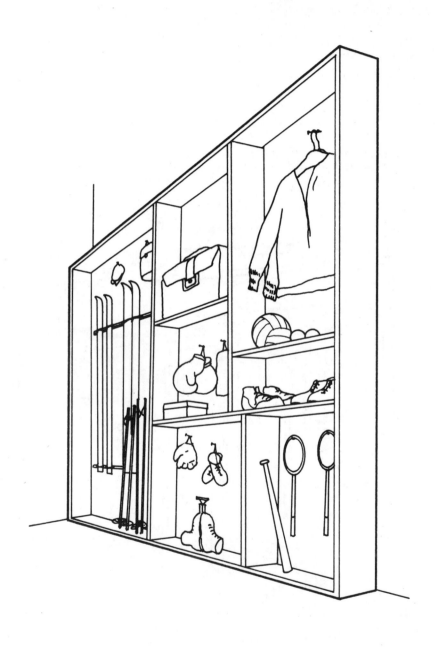

Bicycles can be hung from the rafters
by their frames or wheels. They can
also be stood up against a wall with
their wheels fitted into brackets.

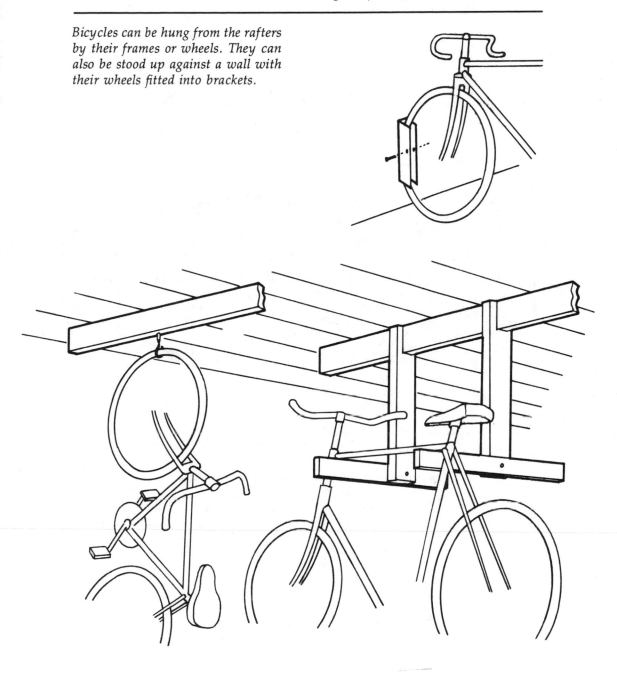

The space in a garage above the roof of a car can be taken up with a cabinet that is hoisted up and down via a system of pulleys.

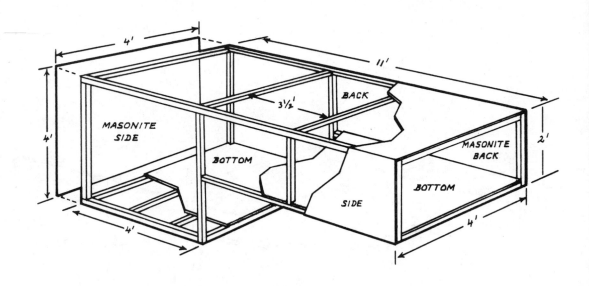

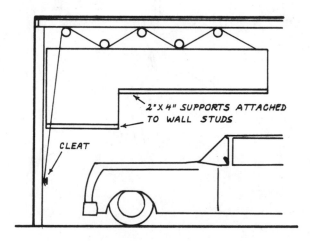

Small objects kept in jars can be hung by their lids from the bottom of a shelf. Long-handled tools can be kept in place by covering the notches in a board with pieces of old garden hose. Bins used to hold soil or powder can have a lift-up gate for easy pouring.

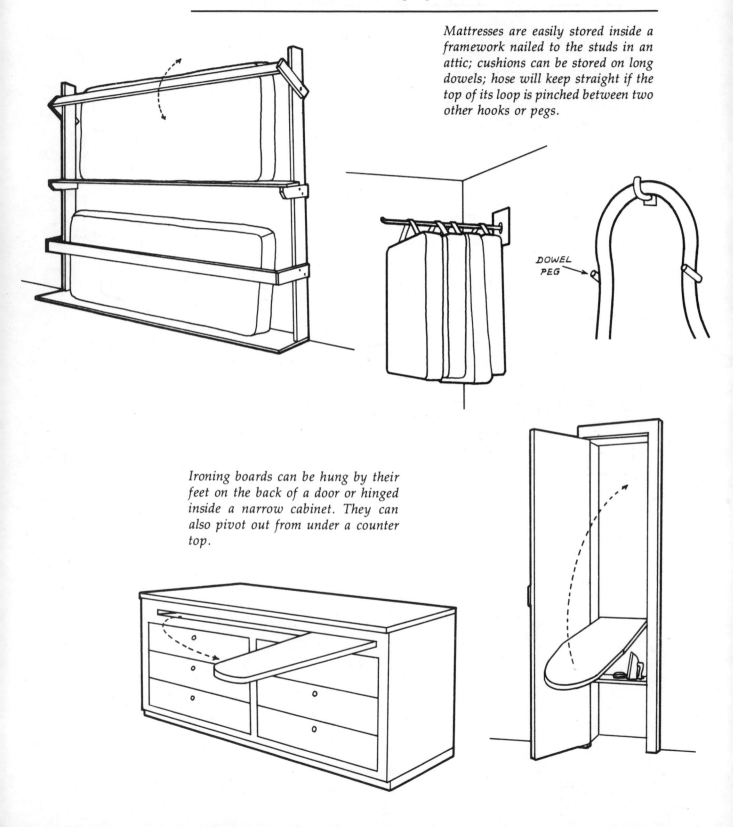

Mattresses are easily stored inside a framework nailed to the studs in an attic; cushions can be stored on long dowels; hose will keep straight if the top of its loop is pinched between two other hooks or pegs.

DOWEL PEG

Ironing boards can be hung by their feet on the back of a door or hinged inside a narrow cabinet. They can also pivot out from under a counter top.

Index